Encounters with the Americas

PEABODY MUSEUM PRESS

Encounters with the Americas

Rosemary A. Joyce and Susan A. M. Shumaker

PHOTOGRAPHS BY HILLEL S. BURGER

PEABODY MUSEUM OF ARCHAEOLOGY AND ETHNOLOGY

HARVARD UNIVERSITY

CAMBRIDGE, MASSACHUSETTS 1995

Cover Photograph: Piedras Negras, Relief 2, Structure 0-13 (00-36-20/C2740)

Designed by Janis Owens
Cover 230 gsm Suncard
Text 105 gsm Taio Artpaper (acid-free stock)
Printed by Toppan Printing Co. (S) Pte. Ltd., Singapore

ISBN 0-87365-815-9
Library of Congress Catalog Card Number 94-066687

Acknowledgments

The exhibition "Encounters with the Americas" was made possible by the generous support of Doris Z. Stone. Funding for some portions was previously provided by the Heritage Plantation of Sandwich and its members. A planning grant from the National Endowment for the Humanities contributed to the development of ideas incorporated in the section "Before 1492."

Exhibit themes and text were developed by Rosemary A. Joyce with the assistance of Susan A. M. Shumaker, and were reviewed by Professors David Maybury-Lewis, Robert Preucel, Evon Z. Vogt, and Gordon R. Willey of the Department of Anthropology, Harvard University. Exhibit photography was undertaken by Hillel S. Burger. Research and support for photography was provided by Martha Labell and Heidi Miller.

Design, implementation, and fabrication of the exhibit were directed by Richard V. Riccio, with the aid of Noelani Crawford (case and mount fabrication, textile coordination), Edward Ferreira (exhibit construction), David Formanek (exhibit fabrication), Joseph Johns (construction coordination), Ross Jolly (case fabrication and exhibit construction), Lee Nathaniel Saffel (graphic design and fabrication), Susan A. M. Shumaker (graphic design and photography), and Samuel Tager (mount design and fabrication). Object conservation and mount-making were provided by Scott Fulton and T. Rose Holdcraft.

Among the many scholars whose cooperation and comments were much appreciated, the authors would like to recognize the consultants who took part in planning under the NEH grant in 1986–1987: Elizabeth Boone, David C. Grove, Mary W. Helms, Joyce Marcus, Rosemary Sharp, Linda Schele, and Richard Townsend; Walter Morris, Jr., and Marilyn Salvador for advice on the contemporary Maya and Kuna; and John G. Fox, Susan D. Gillespie, John S. Henderson, and Russell N. Sheptak for help with specific questions that arose during production of the exhibit. Margaret R. Courtney, Publication Director, and Janis Owens, designer, oversaw the production of this book from its original manuscript. Special thanks go to Meredith Chesson for her efforts in making editorial changes to the text.

There would have been no exhibit without the vision of past museum director C. C. Lamberg-Karlovsky and present museum director David Pilbeam. Professor Pilbeam insisted that a catalogue accompany the exhibit and added the funding to his list of priorities. The authors deeply appreciate their encouragement and support in all stages of exhibit development.

Contents

Encounters with the Americas

The frontal figure on this monument stands in a pose familiar in the Maya art of distant Copan, Honduras. Photograph and drawings of limestone stela from La Paleta, Rio Klaura, Honduras (24-45-20/C9871/N27597, N27730 A-B). Original drawings by Symme Burstein in Doris Stone, Pre-Columbian Man Finds Central America, *Peabody Museum Press, Harvard University, Cambridge, 1972.*

Introduction

The Peabody Museum and Latin America

Before the Spanish arrived in the Americas, societies from the southwest United States to the Peruvian Andes were already linked by networks of exchange and communication. Domesticated plants, including maize, beans, and chilies, were adopted over wide areas. Innovations in basic technologies such as pottery and metalwork spread from one group to another. Even complex religious and political concepts from one area could influence other near and distant societies. A carved stone monument from near the border between modern Honduras and Nicaragua uses the same conventions found on monuments of Copan, far to the west. Like them, it shows a person wearing a feather costume, cradling in his arms a bar that among the Maya was a symbol of political authority. Before Columbus, many Native American societies used costume to mark social and cultural differences. Costume transformed the human body into a display of a specific social identity. It could signal a person's gender, rank, ethnicity, and role in society.

When Spanish sailors arrived in Central America in the early 1500s, they encountered remains of centuries-old civilizations. The sixteenth-century Spanish soldiers met, fought with, and eventually politically dominated the inhabitants of states created by descendants of the Classic Maya and other earlier cultures. Four centuries later, with excavations at Copan, the Peabody Museum began its involvement in the study of precolumbian culture. Throughout the five centuries that have elapsed since the first European encounters, the descendants of sixteenth-century peoples of Central and South America have maintained their own cultural values and sense of identity.

The costumes drawn and described in sixteenth-century manuscripts, and recorded in precolumbian human images provide a panorama of the complexity of social life in native societies of Central and South America. Costume ornaments made of imperishable material, recovered in burials, allowed archaeologists to relate real people with these images. Distinctions between elite and commoners, men and women, soldiers, participants in ritual, and others, were all symbolized in costume. Within the modern states that have developed since the Spanish Conquest, costume continues to be one of the most visible dimensions for the display of distinctive native identity. Costume reinforces commonality within native societies and difference from

Members of the Peabody Museum expedition to Copan, Honduras, receiving local visitors in the mid-1890s. Peabody Museum Photographic Archives (N27/N32807).

the politically dominant cultures derived from Europe. Through these centuries, the manufacture of distinctive native costume has actively incorporated new materials, techniques, and imagery that resulted from European colonization, to strengthen the thread of tradition.

In December 1992, the Peabody Museum reopened its renovated third-floor gallery, traditionally devoted to the precolumbian cultures of Central America, with an exhibit featuring both archaeological and ethnographic aspects of Latin America. "Encounters with the Americas: 12,000 B.C. — A.D. 1492–1992" was a response to interest in the 500th anniversary of the first voyage of Christopher Columbus to the Americas, a journey which began the sometimes brutal reunion of the branches of the human species that had been largely separated for over 14,000 years. The exhibition considers some of the effects of the engagement of Spanish and native American peoples throughout the sixteenth century, as these encounters radically changed life both in the Americas and throughout the world.

From its beginning in 1867, the Peabody Museum fostered expeditions to Central America, including early work in Nicaragua and Mexico in the 1870s, Honduras in the 1880s, and Guatemala in the 1890s. Peabody Museum researchers were particularly active in the study of Classic Maya culture. Teobert Maler explored such sites as Yaxchilan and Piedras Negras, producing a wealth of photographic documents for the Peabody. George Byron Gordon oversaw substantial excavations at Copan, Honduras, bringing back stone sculpture and plaster casts to the museum, as well as pottery vessels and ornaments found in tombs and mounds. Edward H. Thompson's reports on Maya sites in Yucatan were published by the Peabody, and eventually the collection he dredged from the great *cenote,* or sinkhole, at Chichen Itza became part of the museum's collections. Alfred M. Tozzer undertook early explorations at Tikal, along with R. E. Merwin. Merwin later produced the first sequence of burials from the Maya area through excavations at Holmul, Guatemala. These burials served George C. Vaillant as material for establishing ceramic styles and sequences for the Classic Maya. Excavations by the Carnegie Institution of Washington at Uaxactun confirmed this sequence and extended it even earlier. Carnegie staff members had close ties to the

The Central American hall of the Peabody Museum in 1899. Peabody Museum Photographic Archives (N1766).

museum, and when the Institution ended its program of Maya investigations in the 1950s, all the documents, photographs, and collections they had kept in the United States were transferred to the Peabody. Among these materials were important copies by Antonio Tejeda of murals from the Classic Maya site of Bonampak.

These and other archaeological expeditions to sites in the Maya area and in Lower Central America were featured in the major galleries on the museum's third floor. The organization of exhibits in these galleries presented a sequence of development for each area, especially of ceramic vessels and figurines, designed to facilitate study by students specializing in culture history. The sequences of artifacts were complemented by the display of pieces of original sculpture and casts of Maya monuments in the lofty central areas of the galleries. While periodic changes were made to content and organization as knowledge changed interpretations, and as new research sponsored by the museum took place, the dedication of the galleries to archaeology was maintained.

The need to renovate these galleries was clear by the 1980s. Approaches to archaeology had changed sufficiently to make the old teaching exhibits less useful. The museum had engaged in a series of projects to improve accessibility of the collections for research, thus changing the use of exhibit space throughout the building. At the same time, the museum developed a new exhibition program designed to present to the public the concerns and approaches of modern anthropology. As part of that program, the redevelopment of the galleries features both the archaeological heritage traditionally emphasized in this exhibit space, and the ethnography of contemporary indigenous peoples of both Central and South America.

The museum had been active early in ethnographic collecting in Central and South America. In the 1870s, material collected in South America by Alexander Agassiz of the Museum of Comparative Zoology at Harvard was transferred to the Peabody. Under Peabody sponsorship in the 1870s, C. F. Hartt explored not only the archaeological cultures of the mouth of the Amazon River, but the villages of contemporary indigenous peoples living in those same areas. A. M. Tozzer worked before 1905 on the language and culture of the Lacandon Maya of the Mexican tropical forest. Other ethnographic work was accomplished by W. C. Farabee, Louis de Milhau, and A. Hamilton Rice in South America under the museum's sponsorship between 1906 and 1920. About the same time, John Ogilvie donated collections made in northwest Amazonia. In the 1920s, Peabody researchers visited and collected among the Kuna during their struggle for independence from Panama. Archaeologists working in Guatemala, such as Herbert Spinden in 1917, also collected among the modern Maya. Major collections of Maya textiles by Edith Bayles Ricketson and A. Ledyard Smith of the Carnegie Institution of Washington in the 1930s were later donated to the Peabody. Thanks to continuing gifts of photographs and ethnographic material through the last half of the twentieth century, the museum is able to illustrate continuing native traditions of Latin America.

Like the exhibition it accompanies, this catalogue is organized in three parts: "Encounters with the Americas," an introduction focusing on the sixteenth century; "Before 1492," an exploration of one major precolumbian civilization, that of the Classic Maya; and "After 1492," a consideration of the maintenance of cultural identity in contemporary native cultures of the Highland Maya of Guatemala, the San Blas Kuna of Panama, and selected Amazonian societies.

"Encounters with the Americas" documents the diversity of activities that resulted in the colonization of Latin America, and the global scale of its effects on demography and biological diversity. Military campaigns, disease, and

(Left): *A Wai Wai man identified as "Chief Kiwinik" in full dance costume. Photographed by John Ogilvie in 1910 (N4715).*

(Right): *Three Maya women from Mixco Viejo, Guatemala, accompanied by two non-Maya men in European costume. Photographed by George Byron Gordon in 1901 (H8557).*

economics were all factors in the Spanish conquest of Central America's centralized states. The conquest was a long process, not an event, and continues today as indigenous people in Latin America negotiate their place in modern states.

The Spanish encounters with Central American societies in the sixteenth century took place against the background of a history of indigenous social complexity, in scale and nature comparable to other civilizations throughout the world. "Before 1492" presents the approaches of archaeology to understanding the Classic Maya, one of the many complex societies that developed in the region from modern Mexico to the borders of Honduras and El Salvador.

The use of costume to create and reinforce cultural identity provides a link to the contemporary native societies presented in "After 1492." Distinctive costumes are important aspects of each of these societies, today incorporated in Latin American states. Contemporary Highland Maya of Mexico and Guatemala see traditional costume as a connection with the past. Their past integrates European elements introduced in the sixteenth century, such as the Roman Catholic religion, with others passed down from prehispanic ancestors. Today, Maya women's clothing employs designs and styles based on precolumbian dress, while men's costume is modeled on sixteenth-century Spanish dress. The San Blas Kuna, a self-governing enclave within Panama, actively incorporate European products and opportunities in a vibrant native culture. Control of their own land is a key to Kuna persistence, and continued ritual practice, a strength. The peoples of the Amazon also use ceremony and dress to perpetuate distinctive cultural identity. Today these peoples' livelihood is threatened by loss of control over land, as mining and farming spread deforestation. The importance of materials used to form elaborate feather costumes dramatizes the threat that destruction of the rainforest represents to their unique cultural heritage.

With "Encounters with the Americas," the Peabody Museum seeks to recognize for the modern world the pivotal nature of events that took place five centuries ago. Reliable archaeological evidence of human habitation in the Americas stretches back at least 12,000 years. Biological studies suggest even earlier movement of people into this hemisphere. Contact between the Americas and other continents was never completely cut off, and further waves of migration into the Americas continued as recently as 6,000 years ago. Reports in European chronicles of sporadic visits to the Americas were dramatically confirmed by the archaeological site of L'Anse aux Meadows in Canada, dated about A.D. 1000, a short-lived Viking settlement.

But the contacts initiated with the four voyages of Christopher Columbus, between A.D. 1492 and 1502, were different. Columbus's voyages began a century of efforts by Spain and other European countries to transform the native nations of the Americas into colonies. As a result of the encounters of the sixteenth century, descendants of people from every habitable continent in the world make their home today in the Americas, drawing on the history, resources, and knowledge of a reunified globe.

Part One

Encounters with the Americas

FIVE CENTURIES OF ENCOUNTERS between the native peoples of the Americas and newer arrivals from Europe, Africa, and Asia have forged a complex cultural mosaic in this hemisphere. European colonization of the Americas in the sixteenth century began a global transformation. As people moved, they brought animals, plants, gold, silver, and other resources from continent to continent. Almost one-quarter of a million Spanish and Portuguese immigrants resettled in Central and South America and the West Indies by 1600. These Europeans carried diseases unknown in the Americas, and even before colonies were established, millions of people died from their effects. It is estimated that smallpox alone killed more than one-fourth of the native population of Latin America between 1520 and 1584. To meet their demands for labor, too great to be satisfied by the reduced native populations, sixteenth-century European colonists introduced African slaves. Beginning as early as 1505, Africans were torn from their homes and brought to the Americas in numbers equal to or greater than European immigration. Despite the horrifying loss of population, native peoples of the Americas survived. Today, their descendants work to maintain their distinctive cultural identities and control their futures.

Before 1492, the Americas were not isolated. Arctic peoples easily moved between continents. Norse sailors reached North America and established a temporary settlement around A.D. 1000. But such contacts did not fundamentally change European, American, or Asian cultures. By 1000 B.C., independent Native American civilizations had already formed in Central and South America. Central Americans used the concept of zero in mathematical calculations by the first century B.C. The Maya used this mathematical system to keep astronomical records as precise as any in the world. Classic Maya city states of Mexico and Guatemala were equal in size to those of classical Greece. But Native American civilizations were different from European, Asian, and African civilizations. They relied on stone tools for construction and human labor for most transport. Pottery was made without glazes or the wheel. Metal was used primarily for costume ornaments. Beyond these superficial differences, profound distinctions between European and native American beliefs and values shaped the long history of colonialization that began with Columbus's voyages at the turn of the fifteenth century.

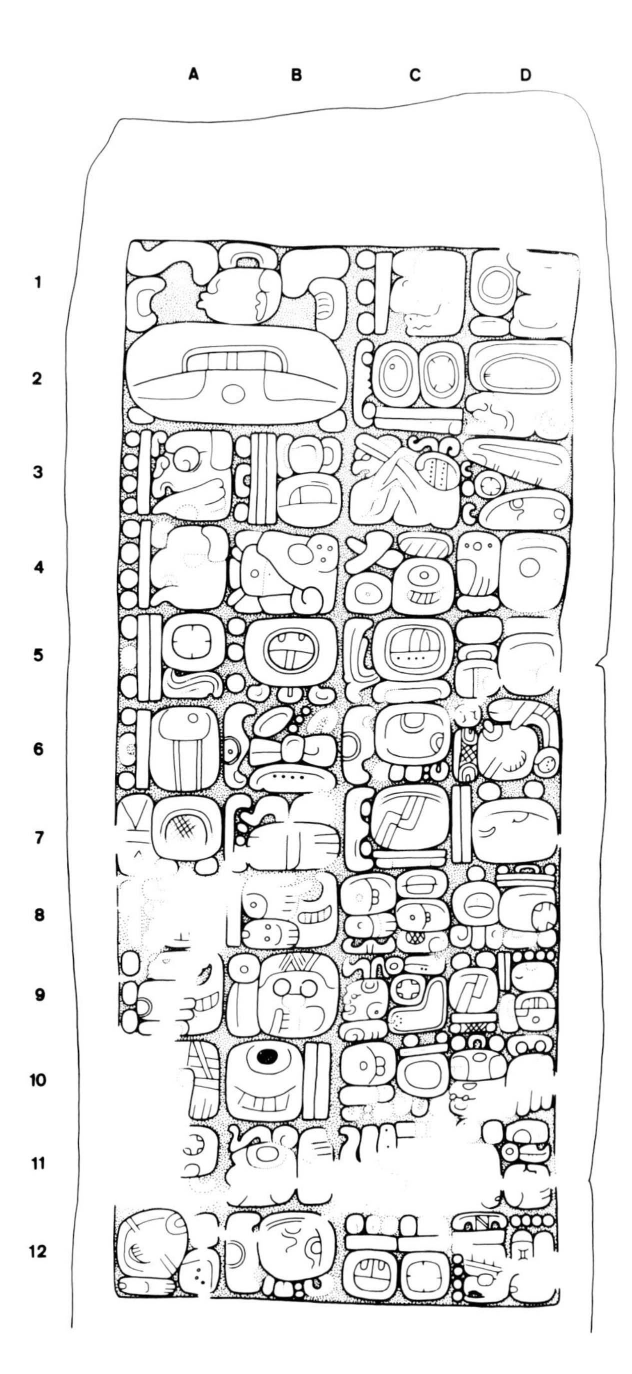

Below the double-width glyph that opens this text, the first three rows of the two left-hand columns record a Classic Maya date in what modern scholars call "the Long Count." The date uses all three of the symbols the Maya employed for recording numbers: a dot for one and a bar for five, and a three-lobed sign for zero, seen in the second column of the second row. The Maya combined these signs to form numerals from zero to nineteen. The bar and four dots in the first row stand for nine, and the three bars and two dots in the same row stand for seventeen. The number nine is repeated in the second row, followed by a zero. In the third row, two bars and three dots stand for the number 13. The three dots in the second column of the third row record 3 Ben, the day in the ritual calendar that calculation of the preceding Long Count date reached. The conventional representation for the Long Count, 9.17.9.0.13, records each numeral as part of a compound number of days elapsed since the beginning of the current era in the Maya calendar, using place notation and base 20 math.

Place notation allows any numeral to mark different values, depending on the place it occupies in a number. In the base 10 math system used in the modern United States, the numeral 2 in the number 200 indicates a number ten times larger than the same numeral indicates in the number 20. Because each place is a multiple of ten higher, the number 2000 is ten times larger than 200, and every extra place will be ten times larger in turn. The Maya used a base of twenty, but the principle was the same.

The value of each place in this Long Count example is marked by a specific sign, found to the right of the number. These signs stand for the particular number of days associated with each place in the Long Count, and are recorded from the largest place (in the first column of the first row) down to the smallest place (in the first column of the third row). The smallest unit is a single day. The next larger unit is a group of twenty days. If the Long Count were simply a mathematical calculation, the next higher place should have been a further multiple of twenty. But instead of having the expected value of twenty times twenty, the Maya modified the strict math by multiplying only by eighteen. This produced a unit of 360 days, close enough to the real length of the year to allow dates to record long periods of time in approximations of years. From this place on up, the Maya Long Count returned to regular use of base 20 place notation. The next higher unit was twenty times 360, or 7,200 days. The fifth place, usually the highest recorded in dates, was twenty times 7,200 days, or 144,000 days.

In this example, 13 single days, zero units of twenty days, nine groups of 360 days, seventeen groups of 7,200 days, and nine groups of 144,000 days were recorded by the Long Count, a total of 1,421,653 days since the beginning of the current Maya era. The most widely accepted correlation between the European and Maya calendars places the beginning of this era in 3114 B.C. The Long Count date in this example would have fallen in December of A.D. 779 when the number of days are counted from this beginning point.

Ixkun Stela 2. Drawing by Ian Graham. *Corpus of Maya Hieroglyphic Inscriptions* 2(3):141.

First Encounter: The Voyages of Columbus

Christopher Columbus and his crew entered a world where they were able only to guess at the meaning of people's actions. Yet on his very first landfall in the West Indies, Columbus was making judgments about the way of life and character of the people he encountered:

> As I saw that they were very friendly to us, and perceived that they could be much more easily converted to our holy faith by gentle means than by force, I presented them with some red caps, and strings of beads to wear on their neck, and many other trifles of small value, wherewith they were much delighted ... But they seemed on the whole to me, to be a very poor people ... Weapons they have none, nor are acquainted with them, for I showed them swords which they grasped by the blades, and cut themselves through ignorance. They have no iron, their javelins being without it, and nothing more than sticks, though some have fish-bones or other things at the ends ... It appears to me, that the people are ingenious, and would be good servants; and I am of the opinion that they would very readily become Christians, as they appear to have no religion.
>
> *The Logbook of Columbus*

On his last journey to the Americas, Columbus made his closest approach to the great civilizations of mainland Latin America, whose riches he had failed to discover and exploit. Coming close to the coast of modern Honduras, he intercepted a large canoe off the Bay Islands. Although later European writers identified it as a trading ship of the Maya of the Yucatan peninsula, the earliest accounts describe the canoe as originating locally. It carried metal ornaments, stone tools, and elaborately decorated cloth. Despite his inability to communicate with the canoe's crew, Columbus compelled them to take him to their destination, where he became one of the first European witnesses to mainland society in Central America. Here on the fringes of the Postclassic Maya world were large towns with well-defined authorities who enjoyed the products of rich craft traditions.

A copper bell similar to those seen by Columbus in a canoe off the coast of Honduras. Quimistan, Honduras (30-46-20/C11005/N27632).

Second Encounter: The Maya Resist Spanish Expeditions

While Columbus made no inroads in Central America, reports of his voyages encouraged later expeditions to the mainland from the colonies that were established in the West Indies within twenty years of his initial landfall. In 1511 two castaways, Gonzalo Guerrero and Jeronimo Aguilar, were stranded by a shipwreck off the coast of Yucatan. When Spanish expeditions attempted to enter Yucatan in 1517, and again in 1518, they met strong military resistance. The Spanish later credited Guerrero, who had married a Maya woman and had children, with leadership of many of these battles. But the Maya of Yucatan had their own history of military strategy. Divided among many warring states, with more than one thousand years of independence behind them, the inhabitants of these settlements resisted the Spanish as they resisted Maya enemies. One motivation for the eventual acceptance of the Spanish in Yucatan by warring Maya was the pursuit of an advantage through alliance with the foreigners. Even so, it was almost thirty years before some Maya submitted to Spanish rule in Yucatan. Others along the east coast continued unconquered for over a century. Three hundred years after the earliest Spanish encounters with Yucatec Maya, their descendants in the eastern peninsula led the nineteenth-century Caste War of Yucatan, inspired by prophecies of the Talking Cross to attempt to expel the Spanish from the peninsula.

Although unable to advance inland, early Spanish sailors were tantalized by glimpses of sea-coast Maya towns, like Tulum, that they compared to those of Spain. The reports that survivors of these expeditions brought back to the West Indies encouraged others to seek their fortune on the mainland of Central America. Descriptions of walled cities and well-armed soldiery suggested the possibility of prosperous peoples to conquer. Despite the losses of the first Spanish expeditions to Yucatan, Hernan Cortés led another, ultimately more effective, campaign of conquest beginning in 1519.

Third Encounter: The Spanish Conquest of the Aztec State

The sixteenth-century encounters between Spanish and Aztec people were marked by differences in technology, values, and interpretations of what was happening. Unlike earlier Spanish captains, Cortés had the advantage of translators. Arriving in Yucatan, Cortés searched for the Spanish castaways, Guerrero and Aguilar. Guerrero, who would die leading Maya warriors against the forces of Pedro Alvarado in Honduras in 1536, refused to join Cortés, reportedly saying:

> Brother Aguilar, I am married and have three children, and they look on me as a *Cacique* here, and a captain in time of war. Go, and God's blessing be with you. But my face is tatooed and my ears are pierced. What would the Spaniards say if they saw me like this? And look how handsome these children of mine are! Please give me some of those beads you have brought, and I will tell them that my brothers have sent them from my own country.
>
> *The Conquest of New Spain, 60–61*

Aguilar went with Cortés, translating into the Maya language what Cortés wished to communicate. Further on in his journey, Cortés added to his team of translators a native woman whom the Spanish called Doña Marina. She bore a son to Cortés and later married one of his officers, Juan Jaramillo. Doña Marina understood the Maya spoken by Aguilar and the Nahuatl of the Aztecs and their allies. But even with the aid of Doña Marina, Cortés' encounter with the Aztec state was marked by incomprehension of the significance of exchanges. Bernal Diaz del Castillo, writing many years later, described the first meeting between the Spanish commander, Hernan Cortés, and the representatives of the Aztec ruler, Motecuhzoma, in modern Veracruz, Mexico:

> He sent two of his nephews with four old men, *Caciques* of high rank, and with them a present of gold and cloth; and he told these messengers to thank Cortés for freeing his servants ... After accepting the gold and cloth, which were worth more than two thousand pesos, Cortés embraced the envoys.
>
> *The Conquest of New Spain, 115*

Native accounts in Nahuatl, the language of the Aztecs written after the Spanish conquest, show that the gifts brought to Cortés were far more important than the simple monetary value that was represented by the cloth and gold. The *Florentine Codex* assembled by Fray Bernardino de Sahagun describes the gifts as the regalia of the Aztec gods, their "divine adornments":

> They were placed in the possession of the messengers to be taken as gifts of welcome along with many other objects ... One by one they did reverence to Cortés by touching the ground before him with their lips ... Then they arrayed the Captain in the finery they had brought him as presents. With great care they fastened the turquoise mask in place, the mask of the god with its crossband of quetzal feathers. A golden earring hung down on either side of this mask. They dressed him in the decorated vest and the collar woven in the *petatillo* [little mat] style—the collar of *chalchihuites,* with a disk of gold in the center. Next they fastened the mirror to his hips, dressed him in the cloak known as "the ringing bell" and adorned his feet with the greaves used by the Huastecas, which were set with *chalchihuites* and hung with little gold bells. In his hand they placed the shield with its fringe and pendant of quetzal feathers, its ornaments of gold and mother-of-pearl. Finally they set before him the pair of black sandals. As for the other objects of divine finery, they only laid them out for him to see. The Captain asked them: "And is this all? Is this your gift of welcome? Is this how you greet people?"
>
> *Broken Spears, 24–26*

Letters to the Spanish Emperor make clear what Cortés and his men thought of the costumes so carefully described in the native sources:

> The people who inhabit this land ... are of medium height and well-proportioned bodies and features, save that in each province their customs are different; some pierce their ears and put very large and ugly objects into them; others pierce their nostrils down to the lip and put in them large and round stones which look like mirrors; and others still split their lower lips as far as the gums and hang there some large stones or gold ornaments so heavy that they drag the lips down, giving a most deformed appearance.
>
> *Letters from Mexico, 30*

This letter, dated July 10, 1519, ends with an inventory of gold, jade, cloth, and feather costume that must include the gifts sent Cortés by Motecuhzoma, regalia intended for ritual imitation of supernatural forces. The weight of gold in each piece is measured and listed. Never understood by the Spanish was the meaning of these costumes. Richard Townsend, writing in *State and Cosmos in the Art of Tenochtitlan* (28) about ritual costume, notes that the Nahuatl term *teixiptla*

> is used not only to describe living, moving cult performers (costumed persons), but also effigies of stone, wood, dough, or simply *any* assemblage of ritual attire on a wooden frame that included a mask. All of these things were categorized in the same way ... signifying a numinous, impersonal force diffused throughout the universe. This force was preeminently manifested in the natural forces—earth, air, fire, and water—but was also to be found in persons of great distinction, or things and places of mysterious configuration.

When the Aztecs gave Cortés sacred costume, they were recognizing his uncanny nature as a visitor from another world and attempting, by identifying him with their own recognized concepts, to place Cortés in an intelligible relationship with themselves. That this attempt failed is evident in accounts of later encounters between envoys of Motecuhzoma and the forces of Cortés in the *Florentine Codex,* passing severe judgment on the Spanish incomprehension of the value of sacred costume:

> Then Motecuhzoma dispatched various chiefs ... They went out to meet the Spaniards in the vicinity of Popocatepetl and Iztactepetl, there in the Eagle Pass. They gave the "gods" ensigns of gold, and ensigns of quetzal feathers, and golden necklaces. And when they were given these presents, the Spaniards burst into smiles; their eyes shone with pleasure; they were delighted by them. They picked up the gold and fingered it like monkeys; they seemed to be transported by joy, as if their hearts were illumined and made new. The truth is that they longed and lusted for gold. Their bodies swelled with greed, and their hunger was ravenous; they hungered like pigs for that gold. They snatched at the golden ensigns, waved them from side to side and examined every inch of them. They were like one who speaks a barbarous tongue: everything they said was in a barbarous tongue.
>
> *Broken Spears, 51–52*

Even as linguistic communication between the Spanish and native Mexicans improved, cultural misunderstandings multiplied. Initially Cortés and his soldiers were welcomed into the Aztec capital, Tenochtitlan, as honored visitors. When Cortés' lieutenant, Pedro Alvarado, attacked the Aztecs as they celebrated the feast of Toxcatl in 1520, he triggered open military resistance that resulted in the expulsion of the Spanish from Tenochtitlan. Nahuatl accounts written fifty years later present this incident as a tragedy:

> Motecuhzoma said to La Malinche: "Please ask the god to hear me. It is almost time to celebrate the fiesta of Toxcatl. It will last for only ten days, and we beg his permission to hold it. We merely burn some incense and dance our dances. There will be a little noise because of the music, but that is all." The Aztec captains then called for their elder brothers, who were given this order: "You must celebrate the fiesta as grandly as possible." The elder brothers replied, "We will dance with all our might." Then Tecatzin, the chief of the armory, said: "Please remind the lord that he is here, not in Cholula. You know how they trapped the Cholultecas in their patio! They have already caused us enough trouble. We should hide our weapons close at hand!" But Motecuhzoma said: "Are we at war with them? I tell you, we can trust them."
>
> The great captains, the bravest warriors, danced at the head of the files to guide the others. The youths followed at a slight distance. Some of the youths wore their hair gathered into large locks, a sign that they had never taken any captives. Others carried their headdresses on their shoulders; they had taken captives, but only with help. Then came the recruits, who were called "the young warriors." They had each captured an enemy or two. The others called to them: "Come, comrades, show us how brave you are! Dance with all your hearts!" At this moment in the fiesta, when the dance was loveliest and when song was linked to song, the Spaniards were seized with an urge to kill the celebrants . . . A great cry went up: "Mexicanos, come running! Bring your spears and shields! The strangers have murdered our warriors!"
>
> *Broken Spears, 74-77, 80-81*

Aztec Society on the Eve of the Spanish Conquest

With conflict between the Spanish and Aztecs in the open, the stage was set for the first military and political conquest of one of Central America's great civilizations. The Aztec state was the last Central American society to be encountered free of the devastation of disease and the disruption of native culture that spread like ripples from the Mexican conquest. When Cortés entered Tenochtitlan, the Aztec capital, the Spanish finally found the wealth which they desired from the Americas. The Aztec empire controlled production from Veracruz, where Cortés landed, to the Valley of Mexico.

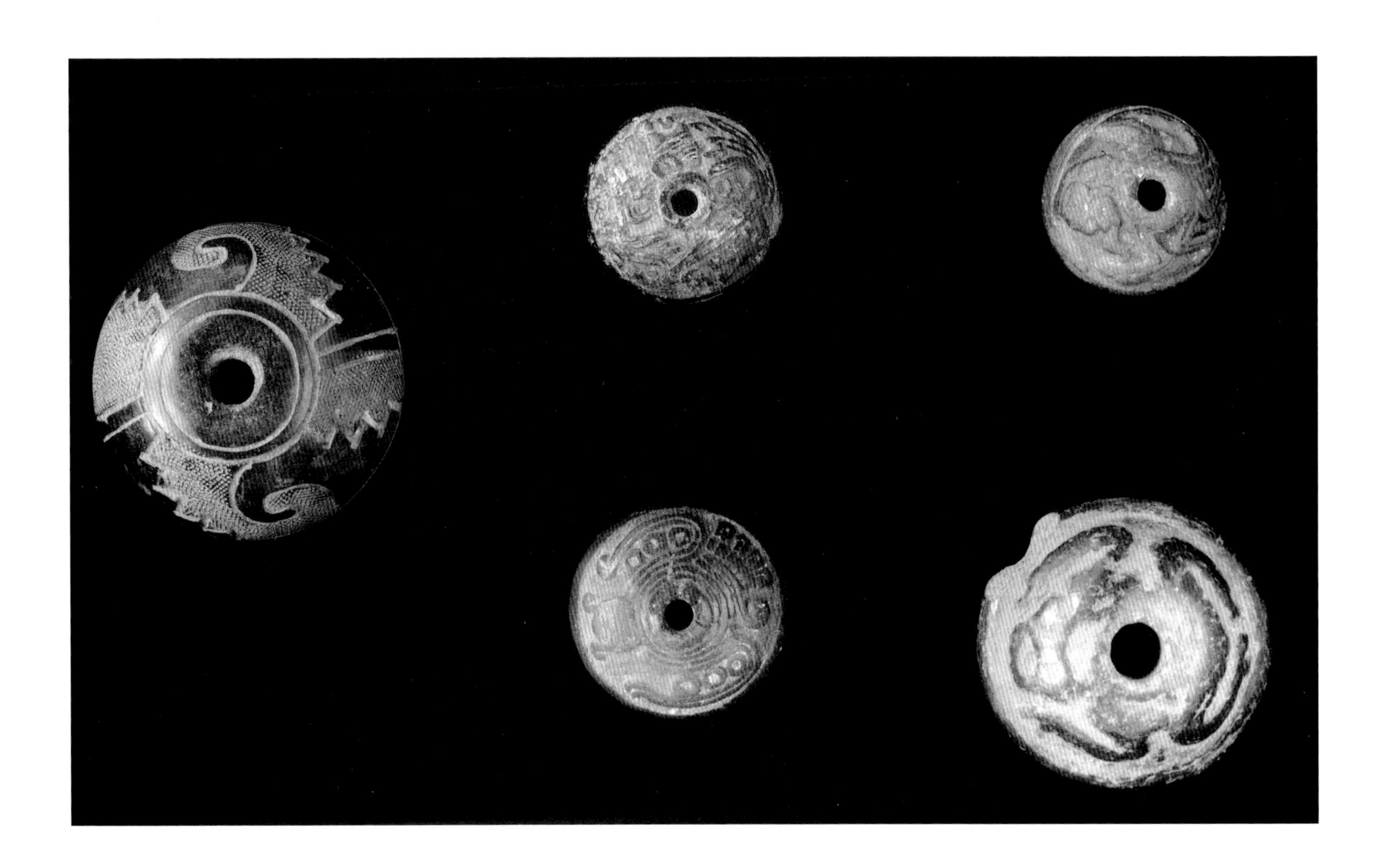

Used to spin cotton thread for fine cloth, elaborately decorated spindle whorls are indirect evidence both of the level of spinning and the value placed on it in Postclassic Central Mexico (N32929: 79-32-20/18780, 18783; 28-1-20/C10104, C10105).

Maize farming provided the means to support artisans working in precious metals, shell, and feathers. The Aztecs united many distinct cultures into one political body. Different peoples maintained their languages, religions, and styles of dress, cooking, and decorating household goods.

At the center of the Aztec state was Tenochtitlan, the capital city, and at its center was the great temple with its twin sanctuaries. The main temple in the center of the Aztec capital of Tenochtitlan now lies under modern Mexico City. Sixteenth-century reports and recent excavations confirm its resemblance to the smaller, provincial Aztec temple still preserved at Tenayuca. Sculptured serpents marked it as an image of Coatepec or "Serpent Mountain," a place of creation in Aztec myths. The dual shrines at the summit commemorated Tlaloc, patron of the rain that made the earth fertile, and the sun as patron of warfare, addressed as Huitzilopochtli. The twin foundations of the Aztec empire, warfare and agricultural production, were given supernatural sanction in this central spot.

The Aztecs used military conquest as a tool to create an empire. Victories left local political authority intact, but conquered societies assumed new obligations of tribute. Cotton textiles, spun and woven by women within households, were major tribute goods. Woven textiles formed costumes distinctive of rank and role in Aztec society. Costume embodied identities of rulers, commoners, and *teixiptla,* ritual impersonators and effigies. Wearing battle dress, a man was marked as a warrior. Wearing the costume of maize, a woman was identified with this vital force:

> When it was her feast day they gave her human form ... And her adornment was thus: she was anointed all in red—completely red on her arms, her legs, her face. All her paper crown was covered completely with red ochre; her embroidered shift also was red ... She was carrying her double ear of maize in either hand.
>
> *Florentine Codex, Book 2, Chapter 23*

As warriors and weavers, men and women provided complementary support for Aztec political expansion. From birth, these roles were the focus of gender identity. In the *Florentine Codex,* native Mexicans recalled the ceremonies for newborn babies:

(Left) *Spindle whorl with image of a warrior, Postclassic Valley of Mexico (20/18780/N32929, unnumbered).*

(Right) *Stone effigy, or* teixiptla, *representing a woman costumed with the regalia of maize. She holds a similarly costumed effigy. Postclassic Papantla, Veracruz (27-46-20/C10039/N32934).*

> Here are told the words which the midwife said to the baby boy ... "Thy home is not here, for thou art an eagle ... Here is only the place of thy nest ... Thou hast been sent into warfare. War is thy desert, thy task. Thou shalt give drink, nourishment, food to the sun, the lord of the earth."
>
> And when it was time to bathe the baby, then they prepared for him all that was necessary; they prepared, they made for him a little shield, a little bow, little arrows . . . And if a girl was to be bathed, they prepared for her all the equipment of women—the spinning whorl, the batten, the reed basket, the spinning bowl, the skeins, the shuttle, her little skirt, her little shift.
>
> *Florentine Codex, Book 6, Chapter 31, 37*

The Aztec warriors who resisted the armies of Cortés in 1520 and 1521, while dressed in costumes of feathers, gold, and jade that for them were full of meaning, were armed with wooden clubs set with sharp glass blades that shattered against the guns and metal swords of the Europeans. But the greatest weapon in the European arsenal was not guns, horses, or fighting dogs; it was introduced disease. By 1518, smallpox ravaged the West Indies. An epidemic of smallpox broke out in Tenochtitlan while it was under siege by the Spanish in 1520–1521. Spanish campaigns for the conquest of the Maya, Inca, and other peoples were aided by disease, which arrived ahead of the military forces. By 1600 disease, warfare, and forced labor reduced native population of the Americas by as much as ninety percent.

Native nobles continued to fight for and win recognition of their status into the seventeenth century, using the European alphabet to write histories in support of their claims and legal briefs to defeat challenges. Born to a Spanish father around 1562, Ana Cortés claimed descent from the royal house of Texcoco through her mother, Francisca Cristina Verdugo, and her mother's mother, Ana Cortés Ixtlilxochitl. She successfully defended her claim to rule the town of San Juan Teotihuacan in the Spanish courts, and lived until 1655. Her son, Fernando de Alva Ixtlilxochitl, wrote histories of the Mexican conquest, emphasizing the noble actions of his own ancestors:

> Only Prince Ixtlilxochitl of Texcoco, ally of Cortés, felt compassion for the Aztecs, because they were of his own homeland. He kept his followers from maltreating the women and children as cruelly as did Cortés and the Spaniards.
>
> Cuauhtemoc said "I have done everything in my power to save the kingdom from your hands. Since fortune has been against me, I now beg you to take my life. This would put an end to the kingship of Mexico, and it would be just and

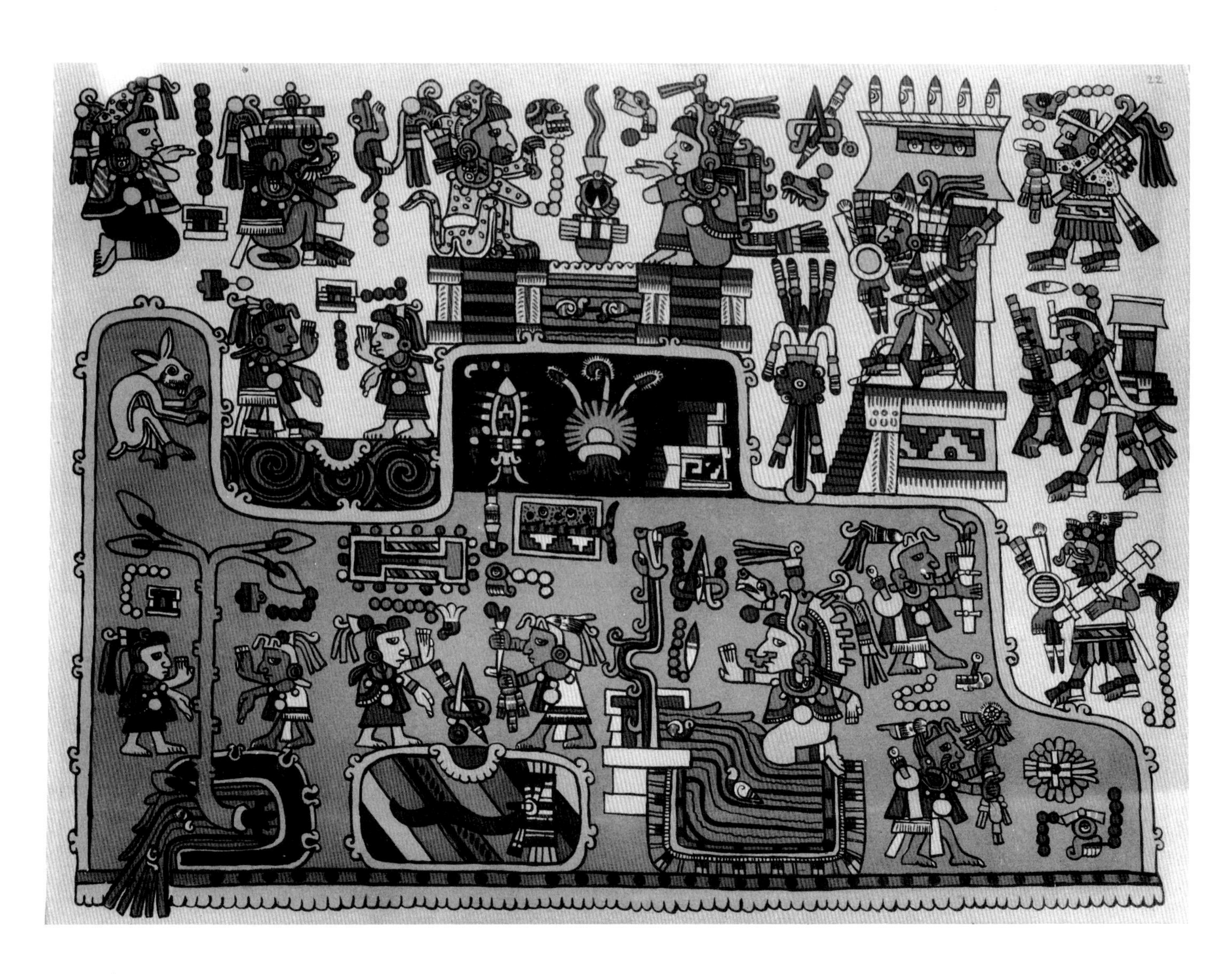

Native historical manuscript, or codex, probably from Oaxaca. Figures, named with their birthdates in the ritual calendar, are shown engaged in ritual and political events. Native practices of employing histories to support claims of political power continued after the Spanish Conquest, with the use of the newly introduced Spanish language and roman alphabet. Late Postclassic
Codex Nuttall, pl. 22 (N22616).

> right, for you have already destroyed my city and killed my people." Cortés consoled him and asked him to command his warriors to surrender ... Ixtlilxochitl was eager to clasp Cuauhtemoc's hand.
>
> *Broken Spears, 122–124*

The devastation by disease of native populations, and the European pursuit of wealth in what they called the "New World" provided an impetus for the massive movement of enslaved Africans from their ancestral homes. As Europeans and Africans moved to the Americas, they brought with them plants and animals that altered forever the natural environment of the Americas and the ways of life of its peoples. The mineral and biological wealth of the Americas, in turn, was transported to Europe, Africa, and Asia, affecting even the most remote corners of the globe.

Throughout the following centuries, European governments tried to impose new religious and social practices on the native cultures of the Americas. But even when a measure of European control was established, resistance continued. Periodic military rebellions followed native prophecies. People were forced to adopt European practices but used them in ways that preserved their own values. Those who survived passed on to their descendants a vital sense of cultural identity.

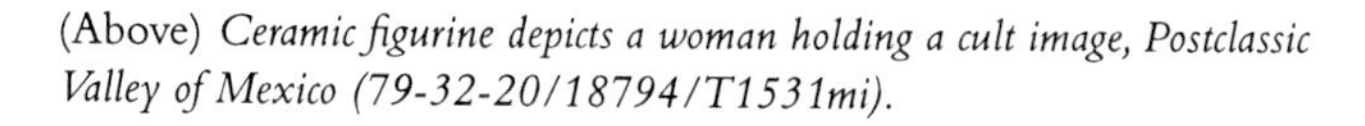

(Above) *Ceramic figurine depicts a woman holding a cult image, Postclassic Valley of Mexico (79-32-20/18794/T1531mi).*

(Above, right) *A tripod bowl, Cholula Polychrome, imported as a luxury in the Postclassic Valley of Mexico (28-1-20/C10385/T1536ai).*

(Right) *A black line pedestal bowl typical of pottery made and used at Tenochtitlan (35-106-20/10286/T1539).*

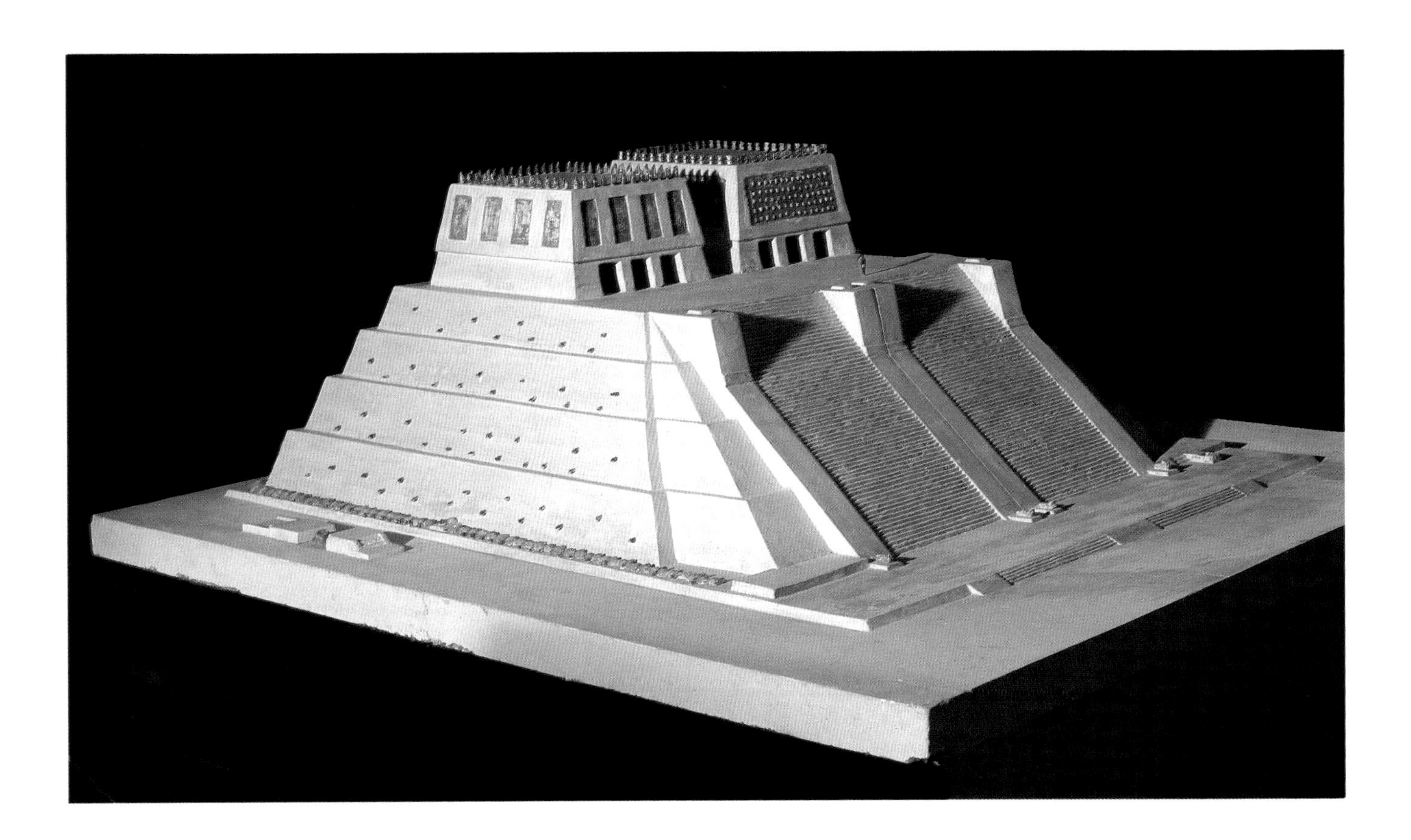

Model of a Postclassic pyramid supporting double temples, Tenayuca (34-165-20/4164/T1513mbii).

Aztec creation myths recounted the story of a battle between Huitzilopochtli and his elder sister, Coyolxauhqui, at Coatepec. At the foot of the stairs of Huitzilopochtli's temple in Tenochtitlan was located a stone disk, carved with an image of the dismembered body of the defeated Coyolxauhqui, identifying the temple with the mythical mountain.

Carved greenstone head of Coyolxauhqui (28-40-20/C10108/T231).

(Above) *Greenstone pendants depicting figures wearing costume ornaments. Classic Maya, recovered from the Cenote of Chichen Itza (10-71-20/C6667/T447, 10-71-20/C6668/T771).*

(Right) *Greenstone ornament showing supernatural being in profile. Classic Maya, recovered from the Cenote of Chichen Itza (10-71-20/C6683/T265).*

Early Classic Maya stuccoed polychrome and incised black slipped dishes with lids represent mythological themes related to the underworld. The polychrome painting on one dish was covered with a thin layer of plaster and repainted. Painting on the lid depicts two profile heads wearing elaborate green earspools and bead ornaments. Based on comparison with other similar images, these heads may represent corn cobs as the decapitated head of the personified maize plant. The lid of the black dish is incised with the body of a jaguar, an animal associated with the sun in the underworld. The modeled head of the jaguar forms the handle of the lid. Holmul Structure B, burial 13
*(11-6-20/*right: *C5576/T1559ci;* below: *C5577/T1519mbi).*

Late Classic Maya vessels depict rulers and mythological beings, and carry texts that sometimes identify the type of vessel, its contents, and the name of its owner. On the interior of this plate is the "Holmul Dancer," an image of a ruler dressed for ritual dance as impersonator of the maize god. The long-necked water birds on the exterior mark the location of the dance as the Maya underworld. The text around the rim of the plate records the word for plate, and names its owner as a child of the ruler of the nearby site of Naranjo. Late Classic Holmul, Structure F, burial 1 (11-6-20/C5666/T1521bi,mai).

Rituals being conducted near a palace as seated elites watch. Early Classic Uaxactun, Structure B-XIII. Watercolor copy of mural by Antonio Tejeda (50-1-20/22982/T268).

A

B

C

The interior walls of three rooms of a public building at Bonampak were completely covered by paintings depicting a ceremonial sequence. Opposite the doorway of Room 1, and extending to the short side walls right and left, the first scene in this sequence depicts a group of nobles in front of a raised terrace. On the edge of the terrace, an attendant holds a young child, displaying him to the dignitaries. The attendant looks over his shoulder at a raised bench where the ruler of Bonampak and women of the royal family are seated. In the next scene, visible on the wall above the doorway of Room 1, the king and attendants are assisted as they put on costumes for a dance. This scene echoes preparations for a dance shown on the lower part of the wall under the presentation scene. At either side of this scene, musicians and masked figures prepare for the ceremonial dance. A long inscription separates the upper and lower scenes on this wall.

(A) *Display of heir to assembled nobles and preparation for ceremonial dancing. Room 1, Bonampak, Mexico (Late Classic Maya, ca.* A.D. *790–800). Watercolor copy of mural by Antonio Tejeda (48-63-20/17559/T1079).*

Immediately opposite the doorway, extending onto both side walls, the central room at Bonampak portrays a battle scene. The ruler and his attendants, wearing jaguar skin gear, are triumphing over other warriors dressed in elaborate feather headdresses. The battle takes place against a green background, away from any settlement. In an upper panel, ancestral figures in circular panels alternate with images of bound captives, placing the battle under supernatural sanction. The second scene, visible on the wall above the doorway, shows the display of captives on a terraced building. The ruler is joined by the women of his family, and supported by his attendant captains from the battle. Above the scene, circular panels frame images of constellations and personified planets, perhaps indicating that this battle was tied to astronomical conditions. In Classic Maya society, raids such as this often took place on dates when the planet Venus became visible after a period of invisibility.

(B) *Battle and display of captives. Room 2, Bonampak, Mexico (Late Classic Maya, ca.* A.D. *790–800). Watercolor copy of mural by Antonio Tejeda (48-63-20/17560/T1051miiia).*

The scenes in the final room mirror those of Room 1. Opposite the door, and extending to both side walls, the ruler and attendant nobles are dressed for a whirling dance. Red handprints on their costumes and bloodletting instruments in their hands suggest that the dance is part of a ritual of self-sacrifice. At the right, the women of the royal family, seated on a bench, pierce their tongues and catch the spattered blood on paper, placed in turn in a spiked cylindrical vessel. Central to the main scene is the partially obliterated image of a human captive held at hands and feet while a ritual assistant prepares to pierce his body. In the final scene, visible above the doorway, a group of nobles stand in witness. Their participation, and the record of it provided by these murals, may have been intended to reinforce the claim of the young child to succeed his father. But the elaborate ceremonial sequence was unsuccessful; the lord of Bonampak shown victorious in battle in these murals was the last ruler of this center to record his name and deeds.

(C) *Scenes of sacrifice and dance following battle. Room 3, Bonampak, Mexico (Late Classic Maya, ca.* A.D. *790–800). Watercolor copy of mural by Antonio Tejeda (48-63-20/17561/T1080).*

This monument, dating to about A.D. 670 and reset in the outer wall of a later temple, depicts the ruler of Piedras Negras dressed as a warrior. Kneeling figures named as members of the ruling families of Yaxchilan and Bonampak or Lacanha have been interpreted as youths, taking part in a ritual marking the induction of the smaller standing figure into military service. Late Classic Maya Piedras Negras, Relief 2, Structure 0-13 (00-36-20/C2740/T229).

Reconstruction of a ballgame in the great ballcourt at Late Classic Maya Copan. Watercolor by Tatiana Proskouriakoff (50-63-20/18488/T382).

Siege and conquest of a village, with warriors capturing civilians. Watercolor copy by Adela Breton, Terminal Classic Maya Chichen Itza, Upper Temple of the Jaguar, west wall mural (45-5-20/15062/T836).

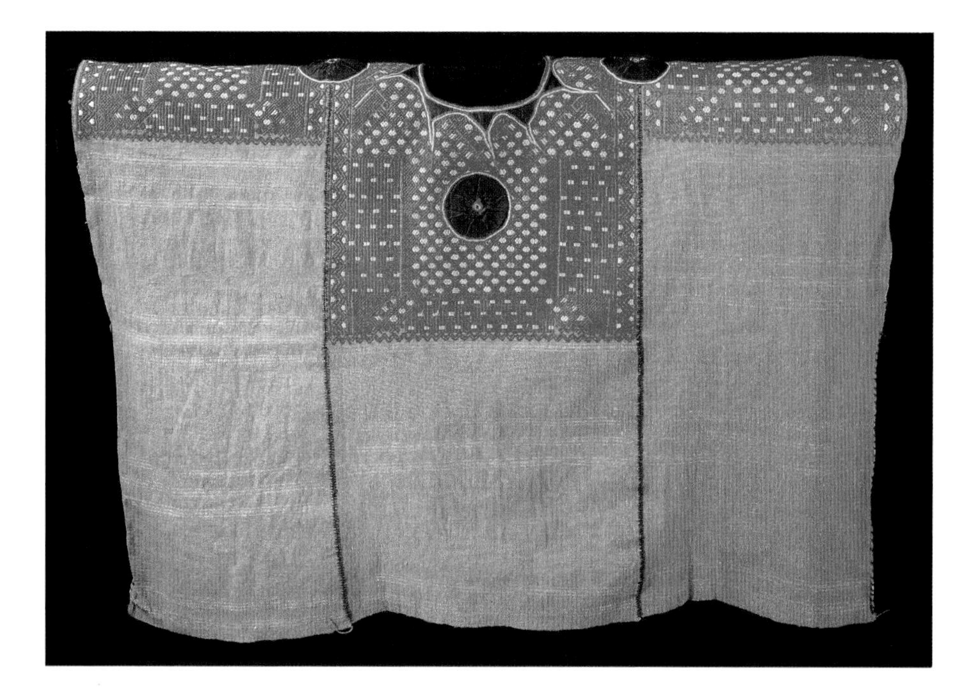

Designs on the Maya woman's blouse symbolize the natural world. Four rosettes stand for the world directions, and the trim of the neck for the sun's rays. Maize fields (stripes), mountains (zigzags), and maize kernels (diamonds) cover its surface. Huipil, *collected in 1917, Santo Tomas Chichicastenango, Guatemala (17-3-20/C7762/T1594).*

Sewn of two narrow panels of woven cotton, silk tassels decorate the corners of the headcloth. Folded diagonally, they were worn tied at the back of the neck with tassels hanging down. Older headcloths have small birds on a red cotton ground, or purple or red birds on a white cotton ground. Later headcloths have solid designs in purple silk. Maya boy's headcloth, collected in 1932, Santo Tomas Chichicastenango (32-37-20/158/T1606).

Maya women's cloths in Santo Tomas Chichicastenango are usually plain red cotton with narrow stripes of yellow, green, and black. The most complex have white cotton backgrounds with red and brown stripes. Birds, spiders, horses, and girls are among the designs depicted in bright colors on these cloths. Detail of cloth collected in 1932 (32-37-20/160/T1607).

A Kuna mola collected at Teguala on mainland Panama in the early 1920s (26-46-20/F577/T1582i).

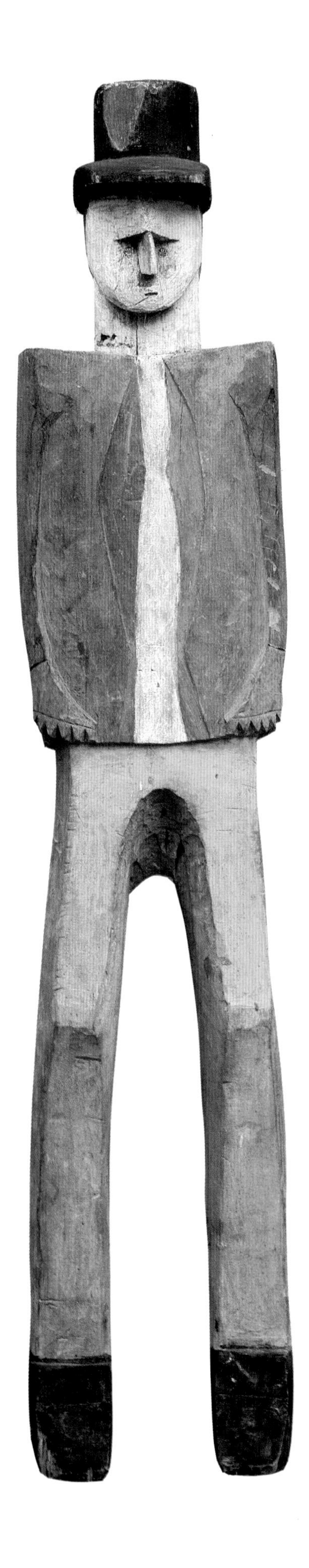

(Left) *Large effigy figure of a man wearing a European-style hat and tie. Kuna "stick doll" for mass-curing (24-39-20/F455/T1615).*

(Right) *Large effigy figure of a woman. Kuna "stick doll" for mass-curing (24-39-20/F446/T1614).*

Men in the maize beer shed, inna. Kuna mola from Carti Tupile Island (971-14-20/23890/T1588i).

Collected around 1910, this Kuna mola borrows motifs from the seal of the United States of America (986-26-20/26162/T1595i).

This Kuna mola from Carti Tupile Island urges support for one presidential candidate, Alonso Fernandez Galindo (971-14-20/23891/T1589ii).

"La Rosita"-brand sardine can depicted on Kuna mola from Carti Sugtupo Island (971-14-20/23887/T1587ii).

A headdress of macaw and toucan feathers. Mundurucú feather costume collected in 1850 (83-14-30/30176/T1597).

Shimári, *a Wai Wai manioc grater board; wooden set with stone teeth (10-58-30/82753/T16290).*

Orowkó, *a Wai Wai diadem headdress with red and yellow toucan and macaw feathers (10-58-30/82827/T1602).*

Encounters, Resistance, Persistence: A Chronology

1492–1502
Four voyages of Christopher Columbus to the Americas

1511
Shipwreck of Gonzalo Guerrero and Jeronimo Aguilar in Yucatan

1517
Cordoba expedition to Yucatan repelled by Maya

1518
Grijalva expedition to Yucatan repelled by Maya

1519
Hernando Cortés lands in Veracruz, Mexico
Alliance of Tlaxcalans with Cortés against the Aztec

1520
Massacre ordered by Pedro Alvarado during Aztec festival of Toxcatl

1521
Surrender of Tenochtitlan, the Aztec capital

1524–1531
Pizarro's campaigns against the Inca of Peru

1529–1534
Francisco Montejo the elder attempts to conquer Yucatan

1534
Inca rebellion against the Spanish

1536
Pedro Alvarado defeats Cisumba and Guerrero in Honduras

1540
Francisco Montejo the younger attempts to conquer Yucatan

1542
Establishment of Spanish city of Merida on site of Maya Tiho

1546–1547
Great Revolt by Maya of Yucatan, inspired by an anonymous prophet, fails

1562
Maya of Sotuta are tried for heresy

1572
Capture of the rebel Inca Tupac Amaru

1574
First prosecution by the Mexican Inquisition

1614
Spanish royal act supporting succession to office by descendants of native lords

1660
Uprising in Tehuantepec, Mexico

1662
Rebellions by the native people of Nejapa, Ixtepeji, and Villa Alta, Mexico

1681
Kuna people independent of colonial authority

1697
Surrender of Canek, lord of the Itza Maya of Tayasal

1712–1713
Tzeltal revolt, Chiapas, inspired by the prophet Maria Candelaria of Cancuc

1725–1726
Rebellion in Darien region against Spain by Kuna and others

1761
Jacinto Uc leads Maya rebellion under the name King Jacinto Uc de los Santos Canek Chichan Moctezuma

1779–1781
Jose Gabriel Tupac Amaru declares himself Inca and leads unsuccessful campaign against Spanish authorities in Andes

1790
Spanish abandon forts in the Darien homeland of the Kuna people

1801
Native uprising in Tepic, Mexico

1847–1848
The Caste War of Yucatan, uprising of Maya following the prophecy of the Talking Cross

1901
Capture of Chan Santa Cruz, rebel Maya capital, by Mexican army

1916
Treaty ending the Caste War of Yucatan

1925
Declaration of the Kuna Republic of Tule

1938
Panama grants political autonomy to Kuna

1969
Death of the last chief of the independent Maya followers of the Talking Cross of Yucatan

1983
Founding of Kuna Forest Preserve

An elite woman gazes up at a seated male ruler. She wears long robes with woven designs representing the earth. The seated ruler wears a brocade loincloth. Both wear elaborate jewelry and headdresses with feather plumes. Piedras Negras Stela 14. Photographed by Teobert Maler, 1898–1900 (N2140).

Part Two
Before 1492: The Classic Maya

Costume, Burial, and Social Status

In burials, ritual deposits, and even in refuse, archaeologists recover the imperishable elements of costumes made and used by the Classic Maya of Mexico and Guatemala from about A.D. 250 to 850. While the elaborately woven cotton textiles, colorful featherwork ornaments and headdresses, and animal skin garments shown in art rarely survive, greenstone and shell ornaments bear witness to the most elaborate Maya costumes. Social identity, status, and role were distinguished through their rich detail. Worn in the rituals depicted in carved and painted images, costumes reinforced the distinction of elites from non-elites. They served as a visible reminder of elite roles in ritual, and elite claims to connections with the supernatural world.

Paired costumes in Classic Maya images subtly distinguish gender and establish symbolic associations for male and female. Women wear long woven gowns covered with symbols of the underworld, often covered by a netting of criss-crossed beads, an image of the earth's surface. At the waist, a belt with central shark head and pendant bivalve shell recalls the encircling ocean. Men wear a long loincloth, ornamented with the branches of the central world tree, the axis between planes of the world. From the belt hangs a greenstone effigy head with three pendant celts, perhaps recalling the decapitated head of an ancestral hero, hung in a tree in the underworld.

The remarkable headdresses depicted in Maya images marked social status and symbolic position. Image may be stacked on image to convey a complex message of affiliation with supernatural beings. Arrangements of feathers in headdresses suggest the wings and tail of a great bird, like that surmounting the central world tree. A cormorant grasping a fish in its bill is a reference to the watery underworld. Political or ritual office was distinguished by headdress. A headband with a profile image of a supernatural being at the front served as a crown. To single out one image from all others, unique signs for the name of a person could be inscribed in the headdress.

While the form of costume communicated gender, role, and sometimes even personal names, the materials employed for common ornaments conveyed

Carved stone lintel showing ruler (on right) wearing profile greenstone ornament attached to front of his headdress. Yaxchilan Lintel 3. Photographed by Teobert Maler, 1897–1903 (N2668).

information about social status. Archaeologists use the dramatic differences given material form in burials as one signal of the presence of distinct social groups. In Classic Maya society, a minority of individuals were buried within public architecture. While most members of society were buried with little in the way of goods, some were clothed in rich costumes and accompanied by objects of pottery, shell, stone, and more perishable materials.

Costume ornaments and tools symbolic of the role and status of elites were incorporated in their tombs. At the Early Classic site of Holmul, pottery vessels with images of the watery underworld pictured the realm of the dead, the new location of those buried. Incised shell ear ornaments carried the images of young lords, perhaps versions of the mythic hero twins of Maya oral tradition, who battled the lords of the underworld and were reborn after struggle.

Social hierarchy among the Classic Maya fueled diversity in the numbers and kinds of items in burials. Plain greenstone earspools were universal among the elite. Other items were more specific. A cut shell paint pot suggests its owner was a scribe. Written texts provide the most specific information about buried

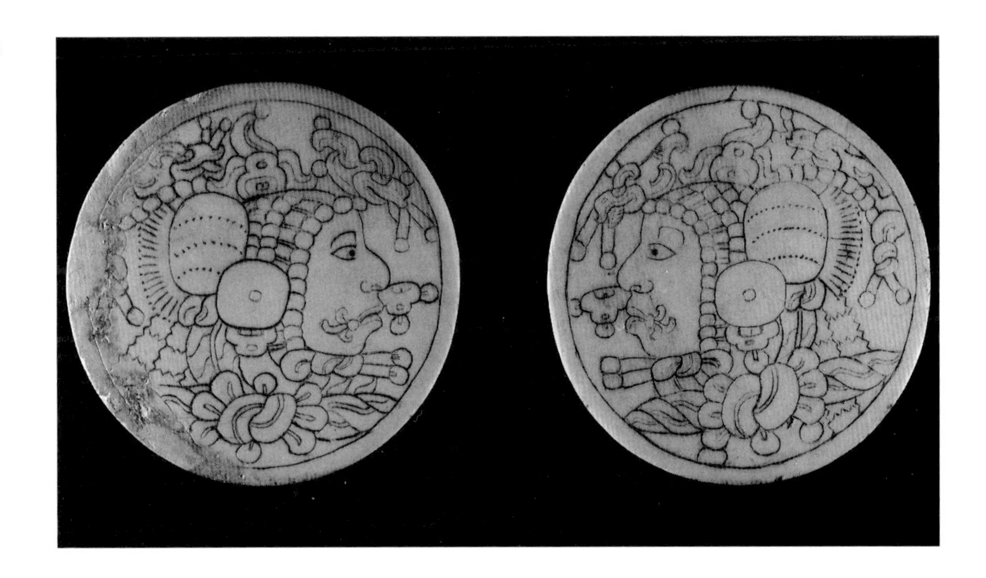

Ear ornaments of carved shell, depicting the heads of young lords. Holmul Structure B, in room with burial 13 (11-6-20/C5619, C5620/ N32967).

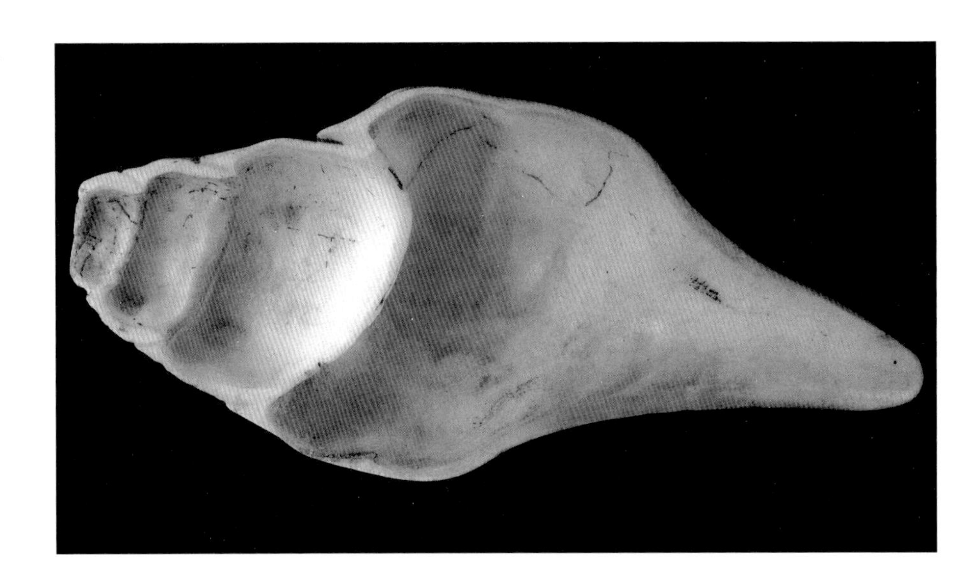

Paint pot, sectioned shell, similar to objects shown held by scribes on pottery vessels. Holmul Structure B, in room with burial 13 (11-6-20/C5610/N32961).

Stingray spine with incised text. Stingray spines were used in personal bloodletting rites. The short text on this spine is an example of name-tagging, also found on costume ornaments. The third glyph reads "his/her stingray spine," and the remaining glyphs name the "way," or spirit companion, of the owner. Holmul Structure B, burial 13 (11-6-20/C5487/N32957).

individuals. A perforator used in ritual bloodletting carries a short text naming its owner and describing the tool as "the stingray spine of the spirit companion" of this lord. Texts on a plate and cylinder vase record their dedication as sacred objects. The plate names its owner as the child of a lord at the larger center, Naranjo, where similar vessels were produced and used. This person may have ruled Holmul in service to his brother, lord of Naranjo, and received these vessels as signs of royal favor. Both vessels depict a lord engaged in a ceremonial dance. Long-necked water birds on the plate are symbols of the watery underworld, where the dead became ancestors for their successors. Royal tombs, placed in prominent buildings, helped Classic Maya rulers justify their power as the legitimate legacy of the past.

Buildings and Sites

The architecture of Maya sites provided stages for the development and display of social status. Maya settlements were composed of public buildings around open plazas, surrounded by residential compounds of multi-family households. The construction of pyramids, courtyards, and ballcourts recreated the geography of creation myths and linked the upperworld and underworld to the everyday world. At Copan, public space centers on a temple with four stairways. North of this temple is a vast open court dotted with sculpted representations of rulers. South of this temple stands a ballcourt, in myth an entry to the underworld.

Surrounding public architecture in Classic Maya sites were numerous household compounds. The basic unit of most compounds was a thatched-roof house, within which food was stored, processed, and cooked on an open fire. In the packed earth patio outside the house, pottery, textiles, and stone tools were manufactured. Specialized outbuildings for ritual, storage, and other activities were placed on the edges of the patio. Debris from the house floors and patios allows archaeologists to identify activities that took place in compounds ranging from modest rural groups to sprawling elite neighborhoods.

View of the public center of Classic Maya Copan. Reconstruction drawing by Tatiana Proskouriakoff (50-63-20/18487/N28094).

This sculpture uses the common thatched-roof house as the symbol for a ritual building. The figure in the doorway has the monkey face of a supernatural being. The text on the sides of the sculpture has been interpreted by epigraphers Nikolai Grube and Linda Schele as a reference to the "vision house of the god," naming a human owner. The worn text on the roof of the house recorded a date.

Effigy of common thatched-roof house, carved rhyolite. Periphery of elite household south of public center of Classic Maya Copan (92-49-20/C20, C21/N32904).

Courtyards surrounded by rows of rooms with benches form the palace group of Piedras Negras. Reconstruction drawing by Tatiana Proskouriakoff (N25579).

A few unusually elaborate households are found close to public centers of Maya sites. Called palace compounds, they housed the elite families who controlled the rituals and political ceremonies that took place in the plazas and temples. Domestic tasks, craft production, and ritual took place in palace compounds just as they did in simpler households. Within their multi-room buildings, built-in stone benches occupy much of the floor space, providing a place for working and sleeping. Elite household compounds adapted the perishable house form to stone architecture. The flat exterior roof of the stone palaces covers vaults that reproduce the interior space of the typical thatched-roof house. Like temples, palaces were often decorated with symbolically significant sculpture, stucco, and painting that provide hints of the values and beliefs that supported Classic Maya society.

Communication in Texts and Images

The richness of representational imagery in Classic Maya society is partly the result of the crucial role that art and architecture played in constructing political power. Architectural ornamentation was used in a manner similar to costume, to transform groups of buildings into places with specific identities. Public centers were stages for rituals in which rulers presented themselves as crucial to the survival of the natural and social world. The use of stone for images of ritual gave these claims a permanent and unchanging form. Monuments presented claims by rulers as given, natural facts, incorporating them in compositions that symbolized geographic features and natural cycles of growth. At Copan, the bust of a young lord, represented as the sprouting maize plant, rises from a temple built as an image of a sacred mountain, the mythic source of this grain. Performing rites at this spot, the living lord claimed a crucial role in the emergence of corn from the earth like that of the founding gods in mythological tradition.

The Classic Maya used complex writing, mathematical, and calendar systems to further specify their intended messages. Signs developed from drawings of objects could be sculpted many ways. Some of the same elements used in human costume serve both as architectural ornaments and signs in the Maya

Sculpture depicting a personified maize plant. Late Classic Copan, Structure 22 (95-42-20/C728/N29651).

Sculptured architectural ornament depicting a shield decorated with a mask with fish barbels at corners of the mouth. The mask is worn by the figure on stela I at Copan. The mask serves as the written sign naming a mythological character in texts about the beginning of the current era of time at Palenque, where scholars call this supernatural being GI of the Palenque Triad. The Copan stela may portray the ruler embodying this supernatural character by wearing his regalia. Late Classic Copan, Structure 26 (93-27-20/C855/ N32901).

Blocks forming part of a text carved with the most elaborate forms of written signs. In this text, the diagnostic elements of each sign are incorporated in the bodies and costumes of fantastic images of humans and animals. Late Classic Copan, Structure 26 (95-42-20/C803, C804/ N32900).

writing system. But most simplified geometric versions of written signs bear little resemblance to pictures of the objects from which they developed. More elaborate pictographic versions of signs were also employed. The head of an animal or a supernatural being could serve as the sign for its name. Perhaps extending this practice, any sign could be represented by a head or whole body. The small geometric elements which identified the particular sign in its simplest form were placed on the face or body, like costume ornaments worn by living people.

Portraits carved on Classic Maya monuments were matched with texts about the individual deeds of the people portrayed. Birth, accession to office, death and burial were all noted. Rulers recorded the names of their fathers and mothers, but rarely any other kin. These texts were biographies justifying the authority of the rulers who commissioned them. The rituals, battles, and ceremonial ballgames they mentioned are our only record of their actions as governors.

Classic Maya elites are represented in these images and texts as participants in a complex ceremonial life. They carried out raids which resulted in sacrifices, ensuring continuation of the natural and social world. Sacrifice was a crucial part of elite life, an action through which they forged connections with all members of society. Through the ritual ballgame, raiding, human sacrifices, and personal bloodletting, elites built their political power. Their success underwrote the elaboration of different settlements. Their frequent failures led to the abandonment of individual centers in a cycle of the rise and fall of political systems.

Ritual Practice

Classic Maya elites chose to memorialize ritual as a principal service they provided to society. Divination and bloodletting, music, and dance were among their ritual actions. Tools for divination, obsidian blades for bloodletting, musical instruments, and fragments of distinctive costumes provide archaeological glimpses of ceremonies. Ritual deposits, called caches,

The image on the round shield normally shows a frontal face with jaguar ears and a twisted cord below the eyes and over the nose. This image is part of the sign naming a mythological character at the beginning of the current era in texts at Palenque. Scholars call this character GIII of the Palenque Triad. This face has also been identified as the sun in the guise of a jaguar in the underworld. Late Classic Copan (92-49-20/C842/N32902).

contain such instruments and imply their use and disposal at specific times and places. Elaborate carved and painted scenes record specific rituals in detail, adding life and color to the mute testimony of ritual regalia.

The Great Ballcourt at Copan was made a sacred space by rituals which included the burial of a *Spondylus* shell containing a greenstone bead and red pigment. The materials used symbolized the watery underworld in Maya cosmology, and marked the ballcourt as a passageway to this realm. Chipped chert and obsidian objects buried at the base of stelae at Tikal and Naranjo

Warriors in battle scenes are normally shown holding rectangular shields. Round shields are held as insignia of power by rulers, and even by royal women. Reconstructed drawing of royal woman holding a round shield by Susan A. M. Shumaker, based on a drawing by Jeffrey Miller of a stela cut into blocks and removed from its site. Probably originally from Late Classic Calakmul.

sanctified the space marked by these monuments in a similar fashion. The eccentric cherts from Naranjo include forms like the sacrificial blades depicted in monumental images. An obsidian blade found under a stela at Tikal is incised with the mat pattern which marked seats of royal power. The blade itself suggests the action of personal bloodletting.

Bloodletting and human sacrifice, actions carried out within Maya sites, were permanently commemorated by deposits of pottery vessels containing the tools used in ritual. At Uaxactun, flaring bowls placed lip-to-lip contained the skull and vertebrae of decapitated human sacrifices. A covered cylinder at the same site held an elaborately chipped eccentric chert like those shown as axe-heads wielded by supernatural beings. Five chert daggers from a cache at Tayasal combine cosmological symbolism with implications of blood sacrifice. The stone was selected to show brown chert at the tip of each, suggesting the bloody point of a used knife. The number five represents the entire cosmos, the four directions and center. Placed along the axis of buildings, caches marked pathways through the sacred space of the site that would have been retraced in ritual.

The Classic Maya presented warfare as a phase in ritual. Texts record the sacrifice of prisoners taken in ritual raids. Warfare simultaneously served political ends. Elite men were shown dressed as warriors, carrying shields and spears, capturing similarly dressed opponents in single combat. Victorious lords took the names of especially prominent prisoners as titles. The importance of warfare to the image of elites is suggested by the close association of raiding with succession rituals at sites such as Piedras Negras and Bonampak.

The murals of Bonampak provide a rich illustration of the symbolic value of war for the Classic Maya. The battle recorded at Bonampak, according to Mary Ellen Miller, was part of a ritual sequence intended to signal the selection of the ruler's young son as heir. On his behalf, his father carried out the battle and sacrifice of captives. Specific costumes mark combatants in battle scenes at Bonampak, with jaguar skin clothing worn by the winning side.

A relief from Piedras Negras has also been interpreted as a record of the assumption of military titles by the heir to the ruler. Symbols worn by each

Seated figure and steps from the Hieroglyphic Stairway. Late Classic Copan, Structure 26 (93-27-20/C871/N28552).

figure identify them as participants in ritual war: an owl on the shield of the central figure, a geometric device in the headdresses of the kneeling figures, and the shells hanging from the collars of the central and right-hand figures. The text uses the distinctive headdress worn by the kneeling figures, an emblem of warfare, as the written sign for the action that took place.

Participation by rulers in Classic Maya raids apparently placed them at the risk of capture and death themselves. While loss in Classic Maya warfare did not lead to the political takeover of the defeated site, it could diminish its influence and thus its political power. At Copan, the capture of a ruler initiated a long period without construction of public monuments. This period ended with the construction of the Hieroglyphic Stairway. Each of the seated figures on this monument originally held a spear and shield, identifying them as warriors. As a piece of political propaganda, the Hieroglyphic Stairway fights the decline of prestige brought on by defeat in warfare with a traditional image of victory.

Ballgames, Ballcourts, and Ballplayers

The themes of elite action in warfare and ritual sacrifice as part of the continuation of the natural and social order were brought together in ballcourts. These distinctive architectural settings varied widely through time and over space. The many versions of ballgames played in them dramatized cyclical motion and struggle, represented by the movement of the ball between opposing teams or pairs of players. Elaborate costumes worn by ballplayers distinguished them in related scenes of human sacrifice, often shown on stone markers or reliefs set in or near the courts. Playing the ballgame, Classic Maya rulers embodied the ancestral hero twins who challenged the lords of the underworld.

While details of the Classic Maya version of the Mesoamerican ballgame are lost, the costumes worn by players are documented in stone sculpture and painted ceramics, and the appearance of the ballcourt can be reconstructed through excavation. Classic Maya ballcourts, unlike those of the sixteenth-century Aztec, have solid markers set in the side walls. At Copan, these markers represent the tropical macaw. Sculpted above the doorways of buildings located above the court, macaws identify this part of the ballcourt with the upperworld. In turn, the floor of the alley is marked with imagery of the underworld. Three round markers set into the court are carved with outlines of cave mouths. Within these frames, supernatural beings join the lord of Copan for one-on-one ballgames. The players shown on these markers wear heavy chest guards and protective pads on arms and legs.

At Lubaantun, Belize, three markers set flat along the center alley of a ballcourt depict a pair of players dressed in the same Classic Maya style. The central marker shows both figures kneeling, ready to strike the flying rubber ball. The flanking markers each show a single kneeling figure prepared to return the ball to a standing figure. Behind each pair of figures, a series of lines represents stepped terraces, not the sloping sides of a ballcourt. Both here and at other sites scenes of ballplayers in front of steps may show rituals enacted by people dressed in ballgame costume. At Yaxchilan, images of bound captives within the outline of the ball suggest that these rituals involved human

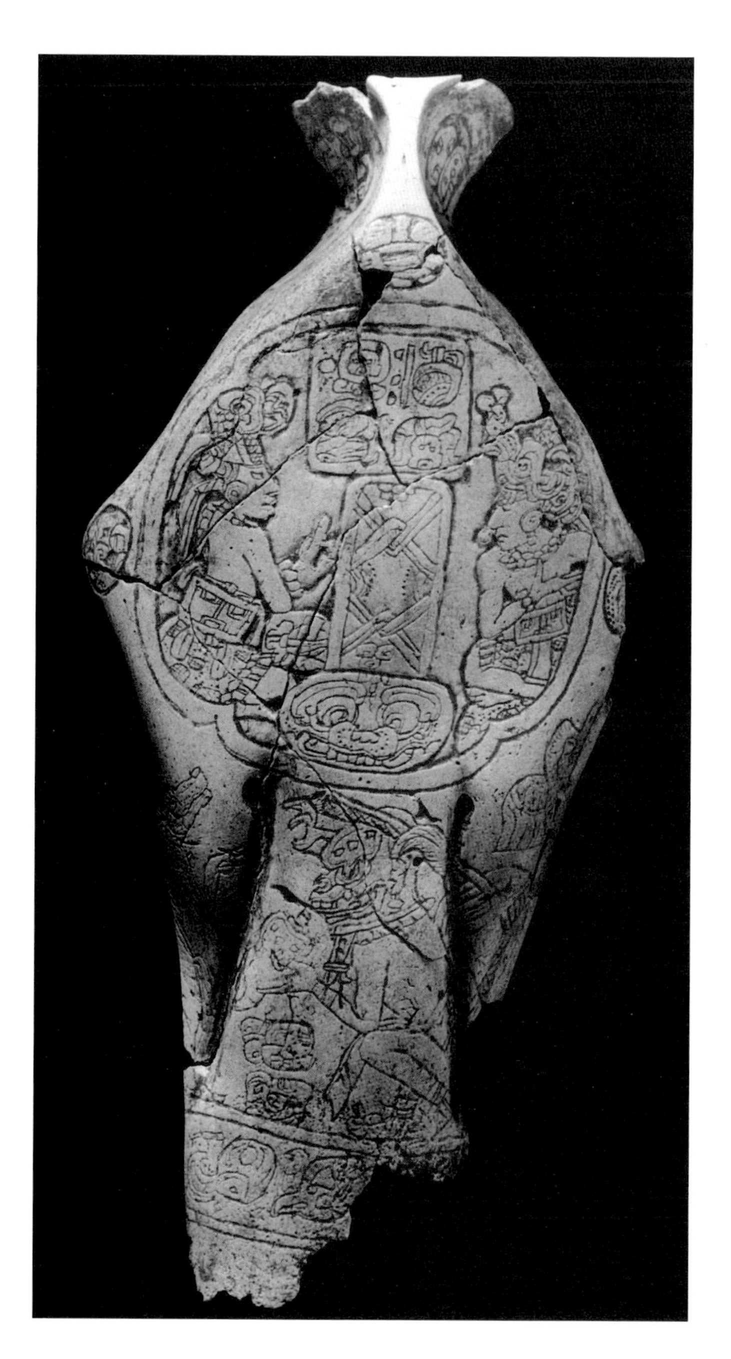

(Left) *This incised peccary skull probably formed part of a headdress. The scenes on it may represent a mythological hunt. At the center is the four-lobed outline of a cave mouth, also depicted on ballcourt markers at Copan. Framed by this design, two figures face each other across a stone stela and altar. Late Classic Copan, Tomb 1 (92-49-20/C201/N27025).*

(Above) *Late Classic Maya scenes of ballgames usually show pairs of players wearing knee and elbow pads and a thick belt. Like most such scenes, these markers depict the game taking place in front of a series of terraces or steps. Late Classic Lubaantun, ballcourt marker (15-73-20/C7615/N32917).*

sacrifice. Mary Ellen Miller, Stephen Houston, David Friedel, and Linda Schele argue that those sacrificed were war captives. Near the end of the Classic period, reliefs along the interior walls of the Great Ballcourt at Chichen Itza associate human sacrifice explicitly with agricultural fertility. Lines of players face each other over the outline of a ball framing a skull. At the center, a standing figure holds a knife and a decapitated head, while his victim kneels before him. Exuberant vegetation forms a background behind this scene of sacrifice.

The Maya World after the Classic Period

At Chichen Itza, established as Classic Maya culture was faltering elsewhere, scenes of warfare depart from earlier symbolism. They show distinctively costumed warriors attacking inhabited villages, capturing the residents, both men and women, soldiers and civilians alike. Participants are not named. The imagery of Chichen Itza glorifies idealized warriors as groups rather than individuals distinguished in specific raids. When Spanish observers came to Yucatan in the sixteenth century, they found a series of independent towns in a state of intermittent warfare. Through raids, Late Postclassic Maya elites captured laborers to work their fields.

At the same time, the Spanish described the practice of formalized ritual raiding between the Aztec of Mexico and traditional enemies. Like the raids shown at Bonampak seven centuries earlier, these "flower wars" took place at an agreed place and time and resulted in the capture of sacrificial victims, not political takeover. The Aztecs, and the less well-described Postclassic Maya, had inherited the legacy of earlier civilizations including that of the Classic Maya. These native societies confronted the Spanish with a well-developed tradition fundamentally different from the European. Their values survive today in transformed fashion in the cultures of descendants of the sixteenth-century native peoples.

Part Three
After 1492

The Highland Maya

> When I learned how to weave, I went three times to speak with the Virgin. I asked her to teach me, to put knowledge in my head and my heart; because I liked her clothes and wanted to wear the same. I studied the Virgin's *huipil* carefully inside and out to see how it was made. But it is not easy to learn, you only see a little and remember less.
>
> *Margarita Vasquez Gomez,*
> *a weaver from Magdalenas, Chiapas, Mexico,*
> *recorded by Walter Morris, Jr.*

Millions of Central American people, native speakers of Maya languages, are descended from the Maya encountered by the sixteenth-century Spanish. Even earlier ancestors of the modern Maya built the great Classic Maya cities that lie abandoned in the tropical forests of Guatemala, Belize, and Mexico. Today, Maya culture is a synthesis of European and indigenous elements. Traditional Maya live in household groups made up of multiple families. They farm common lands and carry out rituals in honor of their group ancestors. Some members of Maya communities specialize as healers. They carry on a centuries-old tradition of divination of the causes of illness. Others gain status through service during the year to the saints introduced by Spanish priests. The mixed heritage of the modern Maya is mirrored in their distinctive dress.

> May you all grant favor to me and to my wife. And in her name I invoke you, mistresses of weaving and embroidery, mistresses of the loom, mistresses of the needle; and also perhaps mistresses of property and wealth.
>
> *Prayer offered by Quiche Maya man from*
> *Santo Tomas Chichicastenango around 1932,*
> *recorded by Ruth Bunzel*

Weaving is central to Maya women's life and community identity. Working with the native backstrap loom, women produce their community's distinctive costume. Despite predictions for almost a century that Maya weaving would soon be lost, traditional textile production continues. In Highland Chiapas, old textiles preserved as the costumes of saints' images serve today to inspire a new generation of Maya weavers. The *huipil* or blouse and wrapped skirt worn by women perpetuate forms of clothing depicted in precolumbian images.

Highland Maya women weaving on backstrap looms in houseyard. Photographed by George Byron Gordon in 1901 (H8594/N33316).

Women from Patzún, Guatemala, dedicated to sponsor the feasts for the Roman Catholic saints. Photographed by George Byron Gordon in 1901 (H8538/N32882).

Traditional men's costume among the Highland Maya is adapted from the sixteenth-century styles of Spanish dress; here, two men from San Juan Sacatepequez, Guatemala. Photographed by George Byron Gordon in 1901 (N28322).

A group of Highland Maya boys are dressed in traditional costume. Photographed on the road by George Byron Gordon in 1901 (H8448/N33313).

Men wear a version of the colonial European jacket, shirt, and pants. Ruth Bunzel recorded that young boys in the Maya community of Chichicastenango wore a small version of the man's costume and began their training for adult life beginning around age five. Girls began to weave on the backstrap loom at about the same age. Prior to this age, young boys wore a simple shirt and headcloth.

> The woman says to her husband, "Now it is morning. Let us get up." As soon as the fire is going the woman starts to grind for the morning meal. Then the man gets up and chops wood for the fire. After breakfast they all go about their work; the men to the fields or whatever work they may have to do; the women sit down to weave. At five o'clock the women put away their weaving and begin to clean and boil the corn for the next day's meals. At six o'clock the men return from their work. During the evening the women spin cotton, and wind the yarn. We say a short prayer before sleeping: "God, protect me this night, and defend me from my enemies. And give me some sign in my dreams that I may know whether to expect good or evil fortune."
>
> *Anonymous Quiche Maya man,*
> *talking to anthropologist Ruth Bunzel around 1932*

A market scene with women using woven cloths. Photographed by George Byron Gordon in 1901 (H8479/N31349).

The central market in Guatemala City, with seated Maya women in different community costumes. Photographed by George Byron Gordon in 1901 (H8548/N33315).

Adults and children taking part in a traditional dance of the bulls in San Juan Sacatepequez. Photographed by George Byron Gordon in 1901 (H8539/N31345).

Every man in Chichicastenango had several headcloths. Bunzel wrote that one of the arguments offered to persuade young men to marry was that their mothers could no longer weave their cloths. Each woman also needed many cloths. Today, women use woven cloths in their journeys to and from the market. Purchases are wrapped in layers of cloth or placed in baskets tied up in a cloth. Even money is kept inside cloth bundles. Women also use pairs of cloths to wrap their babies and support them on their backs. Babies held in this fashion do not interfere with daily work, including the weaving through which women reproduce distinctive community costumes.

Traditional Maya men and women work together to ensure the continuity of their culture through their families. The clothing they wear displays their precolumbian and Spanish colonial inheritance, and visibly distinguishes them from Maya of other communities and from non-Maya, with whom they mingle at work and in the market. The ability of each generation to train the next in traditional values and practices, with the sanction of the ancestors, the saints, and the earth deities, has been a key to the five centuries of resilience of the post-hispanic Maya.

> Hail gum and wax (copal incense and candles), and also you, branches of flowers! You bear your significance, and you shall hear that which is yours. It is your mission to plead before the holy World, and before the saints in the church, and especially before the presence of our Lord, San Juan, Padrino, and Our Lord Jesus Christ who is in Calvario, on behalf of the girl Juana Pérez who is about to receive in her hands her blossoming branch. Today it is five months since she conceived, and if God is merciful to watch over her, probably within four months she will receive her blossoming branch from the hands of God. And this is what we beseech: that death may not overtake the poor Juana Pérez. Now you have heard, gum and wax. If they ask you in the World, and before all the saints, you shall declare your true significance, which is the defense of Juana Pérez in her life and fortune. Hail, Father Christ, and Señor San Juan Bautista! Thou art our star and moon of our destiny. And thou also, Señora María Santana! May your presence come hither and give us your blessing upon our heads.
>
> *Prayer offered by Quiche Maya man from Santo Tomas Chichicastenango around 1932, recorded by Ruth Bunzel*

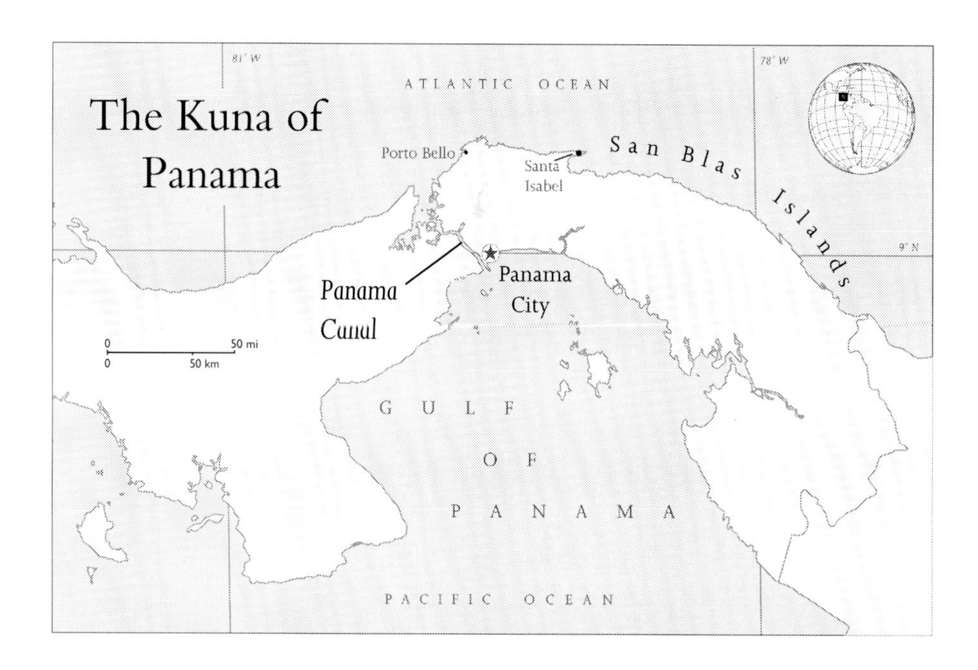

The area of contemporary Kuna communities in Panama. Map by Lee Nathaniel Saffel.

The Kuna of Panama

> Little baby. Your mother is sitting with you in your hammock. Father is not here I see. He went to the jungle. "I am going to clear out the coconut farms." Little girl. You will stay in the house. You will make a little mola. You will also sit beside your mother.
>
> *Lullaby sung by Donilda García of Mulatuppu Island, Panama, recorded by Joel Scherzer*

"A talking place, a chanting place, an arguing place, an agreeing place, a serious place, and a joking place." This is how anthropologist Joel Scherzer characterizes the Kuna gathering house. Up to one thousand of the more than 20,000 Kuna may come together here at one time. Several nights each week, men display their skills as speakers while women create the mola blouses which mark modern Kuna identity. In their dialogues, speakers interpret daily events in light of traditional values. In their molas, women rework new and traditional images and make them their own. Molas record Kuna gatherings,

An armadillo tries to escape into tropical vegetation. The hunter wears a European-style hat (979-27-20/25553/N32993).

curings, and girls' initiations. They refer to Kuna participation in national politics. They illustrate striking scenes Kuna encounter on journeys. And they represent products which Kuna buy and use—often with money gained from the sale of molas themselves.

Most Kuna today live in the San Blas Islands, having left behind the lands in the Darien peninsula that they controlled in the sixteenth and seventeenth centuries. They have enjoyed political control of the islands since 1938. Here, social and ritual life centers on households and community gathering houses. Kuna households are made up of multiple families linked through women who cooperate in daily work. Women with special talent concentrate their efforts on making molas. Kuna men continue a long tradition of working away from their homes. But where seventeenth-century Kuna men sailed on European ships, modern Kuna work for pay on the Panamanian mainland.

Man and woman in traditional Kuna costume. The man wears a European-style hat. Photographed by Elizabeth Katz and Norbert Sperlich in 1971 (20-84/N33175).

The specialist's hat makes a noise like an agouti;
the specialist's hat makes a noise like a collared peccary;
the specialist's hat makes a noise like a white lipped peccary;
the specialist's hat makes a noise like a tapir;
the specialist's hat makes a noise like a rabbit;
the specialist's hat makes a noise like a squirrel;
the specialist's hat makes a noise like a curassow ...

From "the way of the basil,"
a stick-doll speech for success in hunting,
performed by Pranki Pilos of Mulatuppu, recorded by Joel Scherzer

Kuna men's costume is based on European models of shirt and pants. On special occasions, men wear ties and black felt hats. Curers will sometimes wear European-styled ties or carry walking sticks as a symbol of their role. They call on positive spirits represented by stick-dolls, *suar nuchukana,* in healing. To do so, they speak the special stick-doll language understood by the dolls, spirits of plants and animals, and spirits who cause illness. In stick-doll language, "hat" means brain power or *kurgin,* the same capacity that fuels outstanding mola design by women.

> The balsa wood spirit leaders are climbing. They have all of their equipment. The balsa wood spirit leaders are climbing. They are at the mouth of the Opakki River. They fill the *inna* house. They stuff the inna house. The spirits are ready to fight. The balsa wood spirit speaks. "You are going to the place of evil spirits."
>
> *From "the way of the balsa wood," a stick-doll speech from the mass-curing ritual, performed by Pranki Pilos of Mulatuppu, recorded by Joel Scherzer*

In individual cures, small stick dolls are placed below the hammock of the sick person. A pot of burning peppers and cacao helps to ward off illness. The curer chants to the stick dolls. The "mass-curing" ritual, carried out for the community as a whole, takes place in the gathering house. Large balsa wood figures, images of positive spirits, are placed against the benches of the spokesmen. The curer chants to these figures, while burning cacao and hot peppers.

> The women carry in the *makep* dye. The women carry in the *nisar* dye. The women carry in the comb. The women carry in the scissors. They take the cover off the *inna* jar. They scoop up the *inna*. The haircutter begins to drink. The haircutter swallows.
>
> Kantule *Ernesto Linares, Mulatuppu, recorded by Joel Scherzer*

Inna, the girl's puberty ceremony, is a central part of religious life. On this occasion, a girl receives her adult haircut, which along with her mola blouse and skirt marks her as Kuna. The *kantule,* or chanter, sings throughout the night about the origins of the ritual, the role of women, the girl's life, and her new adult name. His chant is directed to the spirit of the long flute, the *kammu.* He and other men play rattles and flutes. During the *inna,* female relatives and friends of the young women tend to her while her hair is gradually cut into the distinctive short style of adult women. They drink maize beer brewed for the festival. Meanwhile, in the maize beer shed, men drink, smoke, dance, and play music throughout the night in celebration.

> They make figures of Birds, Beasts, Men, Trees or the like, up and down in every part of the Body, more especially the Face, but the Figures are not extraordinary

Girls in a hammock working on molas. Peabody Museum Photographic Archives (20-84/N33316).

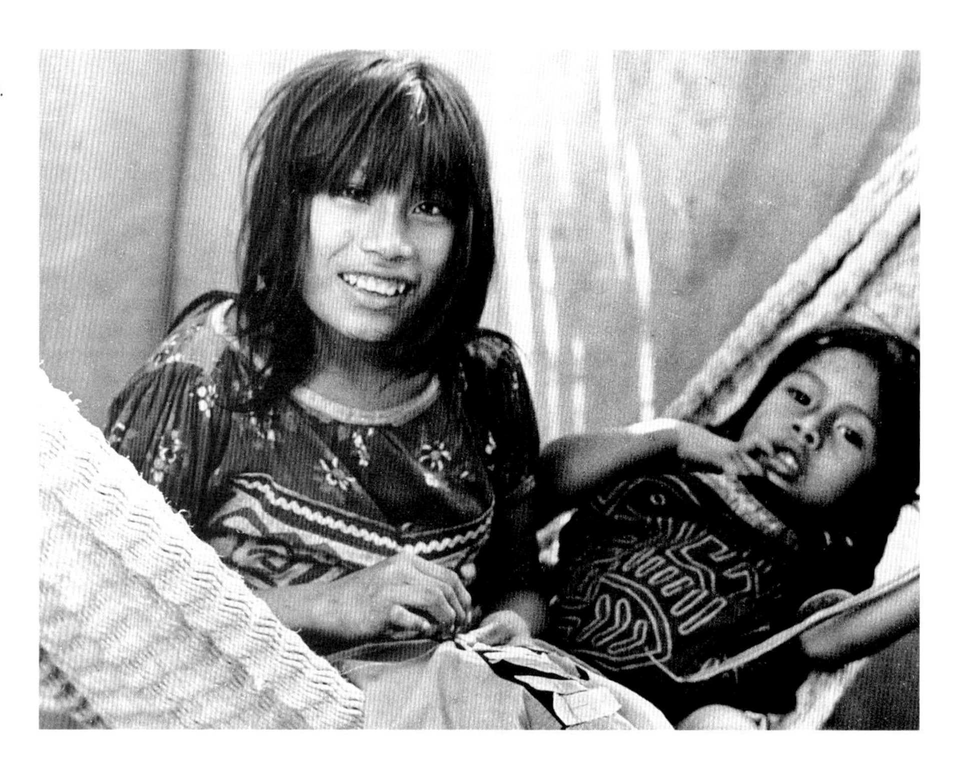

> like what they represent, and are of differing Dimensions, as their Fancies lead them. The Women are the Painters, and take a great delight in it. The Colours they like and use most are Red, Yellow, and Blue, very bright and lovely.
>
> *Lionel Wafer, 1699, cited by Marilyn Salvador*

Distinctive costume for contemporary Kuna women evolved to replace earlier traditions of body painting and incorporate European styles and products. Mola panels are made to serve as part of a woman's blouse. In the nineteenth century, body-painting designs were transferred from the body to the *picha,* or skirt. Later, these designs were sewn on a woman's blouse with yoke and cap sleeves, modeled on European styles. Molas from the 1920s already exhibit all the features of the tradition. In addition to the geometric designs related to body painting, early molas incorporated motifs from other cultures the Kuna encountered.

Today, as in the past, cloth is applied in layers. Designs are then cut out of upper layers to reveal contrasting colors beneath. Molas are described by Kuna according to their use of colors. One of the earliest kinds developed, *morguinnaguat,* features one layer of contrasting color above the base cloth. *Mormamaralet* uses two layers above the base, with some additional patches of color. The most elaborate molas, *morgonimat,* use two or more overall layers and many filler colors, with applique and embroidery details.

Girls practice stitching small areas of molas being made by other women in the family. They are encouraged to learn sewing as soon as they seem interested, around the ages of three or four. A woman's ability to make a good mola is attributed to *kurgin,* intelligence, natural aptitude, ability, or talent. The mythological grandmother, Mu, is responsible for distributing *kurgin* among human beings.

The Kuna prize knowledge of other cultures. Spanish *(waka kaya),* English *(merki kaya),* and the language of the Choco people of the Darien peninsula *(sokko kaya)* are all spoken by many Kuna. The more languages one knows, the better. Kuna culture incorporates influences from other cultures without their threatening its integrity. Both innovative language and depiction in molas serve to make foreign goods part of Kuna culture. Kuna words are coined for introduced objects, like the *kinki unket* (nail undoer, or screwdriver) and *karta muru muru* (paper full of points, or sandpaper) used by carpenters. Kuna women copy even the foreign words from labels of products represented in molas. Molas with scenes of other cultures are women's visual claim to knowledge of other cultures, a parallel to men's discussion of other places and peoples in speeches in the gathering house.

In 1925, responding to attempts to ban traditional dress and rituals, the Kuna declared themselves an independent republic. The settlement negotiated with Panama recognized Kuna political control over the San Blas Islands. Although the Kuna region is politically independent, Kuna vote in Panamanian national elections. Molas incorporate political slogans and images from posters. Following the United States' invasion of Panama, molas with scenes of U.S. soldiers and ships rapidly swept through Kuna communities. Kuna political awareness extends to the importance of the land they control and the necessity of guarding it from encroachment. In 1983, they created the Kuna Forest Preserve to ensure that the forest they depend on for continued survival will be maintained intact.

> Thus there were two ancestors. There were two learned men. These men governed us. These learned men. We follow after them listening to their shadow. A long time ago they were at the Sasartii River. There were many great ancestors. In the times of the ancestors this river was not ours. We are from the place where the sun rises. There was Inanakinya. There was Inapakinya. Why did we come here? The white men were punishing the Indians on the other side of the mountain. Inanakinya came to the Sasartii River.
>
> *Adapted from an historical chant performed by Chief Pinikti of Sasartii, recorded by Joel Scherzer*

Amazonia

> Before you came to live with us, our lives were as always, and we were happy. We worked, we ate, and then we slept. When you came we were glad, for you brought us many fine gifts. And every night, instead of going to sleep, we sat with you, drank coffee, smoked your tobacco, and listened to your radio. But now you go, and we are sorry, for all of these things go with you. We now know pleasures to which we were unaccustomed, and we shall be unhappy.
>
> *The headman of the Mundurucú village Cabrua in 1953, speaking to anthropologists Robert and Yolanda Murphy*

Bororo, Kayapo, Xavante, Mundurucú, Desana, Wapixana, Wai Wai: these and other native peoples built their life and culture around the tropical forest and grasslands that once covered vast areas drained by the Amazon, Orinoco, and their tributaries. Until as recently as the mid-twentieth century, communities composed of extended families supported themselves here through farming, hunting, and fishing. Among groups living in the forest, women tended the fields and processed manioc tubers. In the grasslands, maize replaced manioc as the staple. Men gathered the products of the forest, used not only for

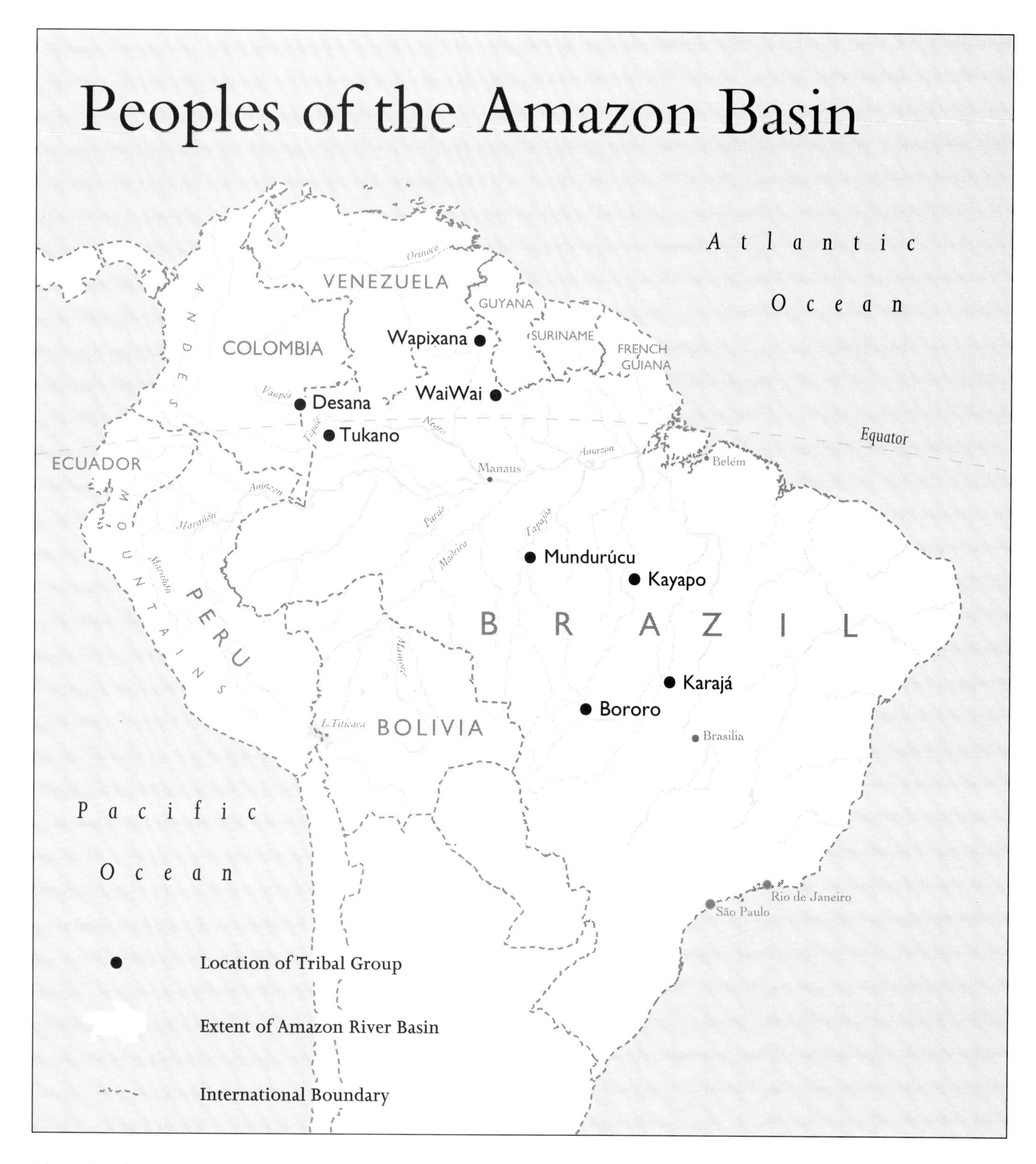

The location of native groups in South America mentioned in the text. Map by Lee Nathaniel Saffel.

subsistence but for adornment. In many of these communities, beer brewed from manioc or maize was served and dancers in brilliant feather costumes performed on festive occasions that drew the community together. Today, unbridled development threatens these native human cultures and the plants and animals on which they depend. Individual native societies may now number only a few hundred or, at most, several thousand people.

> The sun already had his bench, his shield, and his stick rattle; he had his gourd rattle. The sun had everything that the curers do now, and he established the custom of using them. The sun showed how the dances should be done and how people ought to talk when they got together for feasts.
>
> *Tale told by Antonio Guzman of the Desana of Colombia, recorded by Gerardo Reichel-Dolmatoff*

The Desana live in Colombia and Brazil in the northwest Amazon. Traditionally, four to eight families related through men lived together in large houses called *malocas*. They supported themselves by hunting, fishing, and cultivating manioc, bananas, yams, and sweet potatoes. In festivals marked by singing, dancing, and feasting, Desana celebrated and displayed the continuity of the traditions recorded in their creation stories.

Among the residents of Desana villages, some men distinguish themselves as curers and ritual specialists. Illness is visualized in the form of thorns or splinters embedded in the body that the curer must remove. Desana curers use gourd rattles in healing as an extension of their arms. The gourd rattle is decorated with yellow feathers that stand for the sun's energy. The man who uses it in curing follows in the footsteps of the first healer, the sun. The incised motifs on the rattle are derived from the skin of *pamurí-gahsíru,* the snake canoe in which the sun sent the first people to earth.

> The man was perched on a high rock looking down at Urufiri, who looked like an anaconda. He saw the design on Urufiri's skin and thought to himself, "It looks just like the sifter patterns!" It had many different colors in its hide. He took the skin back to the village, and the men learned to plait the baskets with all kinds of colors and designs. Watching the designs on Urufiri's pelt they plaited the manioc press, they plaited the sifter.
>
> *Adapted from a tale told by Fiwi, an older Wai Wai man, recorded by Peter Roe and translated with the help of Yocaru*

Women making grater boards. Wai Wai. Photographed by John Ogilvie in 1910 (left: *N4753;* below: *N4751).*

Chief Yofana making a feather headdress. Wai Wai. Photographed by John Ogilvie in 1910 (N4709).

The Wai Wai inhabit the territory on the borders between Brazil and Guyana. They combine hunting, fishing, and the cultivation of manioc for subsistence. In 1991, they numbered about 1,200 people. Traditionally, elaborate feather costumes were worn during village festivals attended by the people of neighboring communities. These festivals have been expanded in larger concentrated settlements today, with different neighborhoods acting as hosts and guests. They are held not only at key points in the agricultural cycle, but to coincide with the Christian festivals introduced by missionaries.

Beauty comes from the forest in Amazonia. Wai Wai wear feather and bead decoration every day, and apply intricate designs in red and black paint to the body. The geometric patterns and feathers used to adorn the body and crafted objects are inspired by forest animals and spirits. Patterns derived from the skin of the mythical anaconda link manufactured objects to the forest. Even the structure of the forest is mimicked in Wai Wai dance costume. Layers of feathers from harpy eagles living in the uppermost canopy of the tropical forest; from toucans and macaws dwelling in the lower branches; and from curassow, existing on the earth's surface, make the dancer a model of the whole forest. Wai Wai believe that like people, powerful supernatural beings wear beautiful costumes. The sun's radiance stems from the red macaw feather diadem he wears. Wai Wai ritual specialists invoke the fire of the sun's macaw-feather diadem to dry up floodwaters, laying out their own red diadems and saying, "Behold, Sun, here are your adornments so that you can shine." Humans, animals, and supernatural beings form one community sharing standards of beauty.

(Above) *Drinking manioc beer. Wai Wai. Photographed by John Ogilvie in 1910 (N4736).*

(Right) *Wai Wai man in full dance costume. Photographed by John Ogilvie in 1910 (N4730).*

Men dancing in costume. Wai Wai. Photographed by John Ogilvie in 1910
*(*right: *H10316/N4732;* below: *N4735).*

The Future

> The miners came to our communities feigning friendship. They lied to us, they tricked us Indians, and we were taken in. Then their numbers grew. Many more arrived, and they began bringing in machinery that polluted the river. The pollution killed the fish and the shrimp, everything that lived in our rivers.
>
> *Davi Kopenawa Yanomami, Yanomami, Brazil*

Mining, logging, damming, ranching, and misguided farming destroy hundreds of acres of Amazonian rain forest each day. Lands that were home to indigenous people for generations are lost to outsiders who bring pollution, disease, and brutality. In Brazil alone, one Indian tribe has disappeared each year since 1900. When tribes die out, entire cultures vanish, along with their languages and ways of understanding the world.

> Our situation is an emergency. If we don't fight now, we will soon have no land, no culture, no traditions.
>
> *Eliana Potiguara, Potiguara, Brazil,*
> *President and founder of the*
> *Indigenous Women's Educational Group (GRUMIN)*

Faced with threats to their lands, culture, and lives, indigenous people are fighting back, organizing and forming alliances with other forest dwellers and activists. The success of the efforts of rain forest peoples to control their own future depends in large part on whether the world hears their voices and responds.

> We don't need your electricity. Electricity won't give us food ... We need our forests to hunt and gather in. We don't want your dam. Everything you tell us is a lie.
>
> *Kayapo woman to Brazilian official*

For five centuries, the indigenous peoples of Central and South America have waged a battle to maintain their lands, their lives, and opportunities for their children. Today, these struggles continue throughout the Americas, the legacy of the sixteenth-century encounter of European and native American cultures.

For Further Reading

Part One Encounters with the Americas

General information presented in this section about the consequences of the European encounters with the Americas is drawn from the following sources:

Crosby, Alfred W., Jr.
1972 *The Columbian Exchange: Biological and Cultural Consequences of 1492.* Greenwood Press, Westport, Connecticut.

Denevan, William
1976 *The Native Population of the Americas in 1492.* University of Wisconsin Press, Madison.

Foster, Nelson, and Linda Cordell
1992 *Chilies to Chocolate: Food the Americas Gave the World.* University of Arizona Press, Tucson.

Viola, Herman, and Carolyn Margolis, eds.
1991 *Seeds of Change: A Quincentennial Commemoration.* Smithsonian Institution Press, Washington.

Descriptions of the first voyage of Christopher Columbus, and his encounter with a trading canoe off the coast of Honduras on his last trip, can be found in:

Edwards, C. R.
1978 "Precolumbian maritime trade in Mesoamerica," in *Mesoamerican Communication Routes and Cultural Contacts*, Thomas Lee and Carlos Navarrete, eds., pp. 199–209. New World Archaeological Foundation Paper 40, Salt Lake City.

Fuson, Robert H., trans.
1987 *The Log of Christopher Columbus.* International Marine Publishing Company, Camden, Maine.

Accounts of the history of Maya resistance to and rebellions against Spanish rule include the following historical studies:

Clendinnen, Inga
1987 *Ambivalent Conquests: Maya and Spaniard in Yucatan, 1517–1570.* Cambridge University Press, Cambridge.

Reed, Nelson
1964 *The Caste War of Yucatan.* Stanford University Press, Stanford.

Sullivan, Paul
1963 *Unfinished Conversations: Mayas and Foreigners Between Two Wars*. University of California Press, Berkeley.

In addition, two fictionalized accounts of Maya uprisings add another perspective on the long history of European and native relations:

Abreu Gómez, Ermilo
1979 *Canek: History and Legend of a Maya Hero*. Trans. Mario Dávila and Carter Wilson. University of California Press, Berkeley.

Wilson, Carter
1972 *A Green Tree and a Dry Tree*. Macmillan, New York.

Quotations in the text were drawn from the following first-hand descriptions of native and Spanish actions during the initial colonization of Mexico and Guatemala:

Cortés, Hernan
1986 *Letters from Mexico*. Trans. and ed. Anthony Pagden. Yale University Press, New Haven.

Diaz del Castillo, Bernal
1963 *The Conquest of New Spain*. Trans. J. M. Cohen. Penguin Books, London.

Leon Portilla, Miguel, ed.
1993 *The Broken Spears: The Aztec Account of the Conquest of Mexico*. 2d ed. Beacon Press, Boston.

Aztec conceptions of costume and sacredness are discussed in:

Townsend, Richard
1979 *State and Cosmos in the Art of Tenochtitlan*. Dumbarton Oaks Studies in Pre-Columbian Art and Archaeology, Number 20, Washington.

Among the most important sources on Aztec society has been the sixteenth–century descriptions in Nahuatl assembled by the Spanish friar, Bernardino de Sahagun. These have been translated into English as:

Anderson, Arthur, and Charles Dibble, trans.
1950-1982 *Florentine Codex*. (12 volumes). University of Utah Press and School of American Research, Salt Lake City.

For an up-to-date introduction to Aztec archaeology and art history, see:

Townsend, Richard
1992 *The Aztecs.* Thames and Hudson, London.

The Maya text illustrated in this section is part of the following series, edited by Ian Graham:

Corpus of Maya Hieroglyphic Inscriptions. Peabody Museum of Archaeology and Ethnology, Harvard University, Cambridge.

Part Two Before 1492: The Classic Maya

General introductions to Classic Maya archaeology and art history include the following:

Hammond, Norman
1988 *Ancient Maya Civilization. 2d ed.* Rutgers University Press, New Brunswick, New Jersey.

Henderson, John S.
1981 *The World of the Ancient Maya.* Cornell University Press, Ithaca.

Morley, Sylvanus G., George Brainerd, and Robert Sharer
1983 *The Ancient Maya, 4th ed.* Stanford University Press, Stanford.

Schele, Linda, and Mary Ellen Miller
1986 *The Blood of Kings.* Kimball Art Museum, Fort Worth.

Specific ideas presented in this section are based in part on these sources:

Coggins, Clemency
1984 "Murals in the Upper Temple of the Jaguars, Chichen Itza," in *Cenote of Sacrifice: Maya Treasures from the Sacred Well at Chichen Itza,* Clemency Chase and Orrin Shane, eds., pp. 157–166. University of Texas Press, Austin.

Joyce, Rosemary
1992 "Classic Maya images of gender and labor," in *Exploring Gender Through Archaeology: Selected Papers from the 1991 Boone Conference,* Cheryl Claessen,

ed., pp. 63–70. *Monographs in World Archaeology,* No. 11. Prehistory Press, Madison, Wisconsin.

Miller, Jeffrey
1974 "Notes on a stela pair probably from Calakmul, Campeche, Mexico," in *Primera Mesa Redonda de Palenque Part 1,* Merle Greene Robertson, ed., pp. 149–161. The Robert Louis Stevenson School, Pebble Beach, California.

Miller, Mary Ellen
1986 *The Murals of Bonampak.* Princeton University Press, Princeton.

Miller, Mary Ellen, and Stephen Houston
1987 "The Classic Maya ballgame and its architectural setting: A study in relations between text and image." RES 14:47–66. Peabody Museum of Archaeology and Ethnology, Harvard University, Cambridge.

Reents-Budet, Dorie
1986 "Inter-site dynastic relations recorded on a plate from Holmul, Guatemala." *Estudios de Cultura Maya* 16:149–166. Mexico.

For more information on reading Maya texts, see:

Culbert, T. Patrick
1991 *Classic Maya Political History: Hieroglyphic and Archaeological Evidence.* Cambridge University Press, Cambridge.

Houston, Stephen D.
1989 *Maya Glyphs.* Reading the Past. University of California Press and the British Museum, Berkeley.

Part Three After 1492

The following works were consulted in the development of this section of the exhibit, and are the sources for quotations:

Maya:

Bunzel, Ruth
1952 *Chichicastenango: A Guatemalan Village.* J. J. Augustin, Locust Valley, New York.

Morris, Walter F., Jr.
1987 *Living Maya.* Harry N. Abrams, Inc., New York.

Kuna:

Salvador, Mari Lyn
1978 *Yer Dailege! Kuna Women's Art.* University of New Mexico Press, Albuquerque.

Sherzer, Joel
1983 *Kuna Ways of Speaking: An Ethnographic Perspective.* University of Texas Press, Austin.

Amazon:

Fock, Niels
1963 *Waiwai: Religion and Society of an Amazonian Tribe.* The National Museum, Copenhagen.

Howard, Catherine V.
1991 "Fragments of the Heavens: Feathers as Ornaments Among the Waiwai," in *The Gift of Birds.* Ruben E. Reina and Kenneth M. Kensinger, eds., pp. 50–59. University Museum, University of Pennsylvania, Philadelphia.

Murphy, Robert
1958 *Mundurucu Religion.* University of California Press, Berkeley.

Murphy, Yolanda, and Robert Murphy
1974 *Women of the Forest.* Columbia University Press, New York.

Reichel-Dolmatoff, Gerardo
1917 *Amazonian Cosmos: the Sexual and Religious Symbolism of the Tukano Indians.* University of Chicago Press, Chicago.

Roe, Peter
1989 "Of Rainbow Dragons and the Origins of Designs: Waiwai and Shipibo Ronin Ehua." LAILJ 5:1.

Yde, Jens
1965 *Material Culture of the Waiwái.* The National Museum, Copenhagen.

The Future:

Cultural Survival Quarterly. Cultural Survival, Cambridge, Massachusetts.